Geography Matters

SCOTLAND 2

Series Editor:

John Hopkin

Editor:

Philip Duffy

Authors:

Nicola Arber, Bournville School, Birmingham, with Jill Sim and Rachel McCarthy

Heather Blades, Deepings School, Peterborough

Rob Bowden, Development Education Centre, Birmingham

Lisa James, Cockshut Hill School, Birmingham

Sue Lomas, *formerly at* Henbury High School, Macclesfield

Garrett Nagle, St Edward's School, Oxford

Chris Ryan, *formerly at* Heston Community School, London

Roger Sanders, Sir John Talbot's School, Whitchurch

Linda Thompson, *formerly at* Sandbach School, Sandbach

Paul Thompson, Ounsdale High School, Wolverhampton

Heinemann Educational Publishers
Halley Court, Jordan Hill, Oxford, OX2 8EJ
Part of Harcourt Education

Heinemann is a registered trademark of Harcourt Education Limited

© Nicola Arber, Heather Blades, Rob Bowden, Philip Duffy, Lisa James, Sue Lomas, Rachel McCarthy, Garrett Nagle, Chris Ryan, Roger Sanders, Jill Sim, Linda Thompson, Paul Thompson, 2002

First published 2002

06 05 04 03 02

10 9 8 7 6 5 4 3 2 1

ISBN 0 435 35544 9

Copyright notice

Edited by Caroline Hannan

Index supplied by Indexing Specialists

Designed, produced and illustrated by Gecko Ltd, Bicester, Oxon

Illustrated by Chris Rothero, John Storey and Geoff Ward

Original illustrations © Harcourt Education Limited 2002

Printed and bound in Spain by Edelvives

Acknowledgements

Every effort has been made to contact copyright holders of material reproduced in this book. Any omissions will be rectified in subsequent printings if notice is given to the publishers.

Photographs

p. 4 B: Britain on View, C: FLPA/W Broadhurst, D: Scottish Viewpoint/Paul Tomkins; **p. 5** A: Stone, D: Bubbles; **p. 10** A, E & I: The Stock Market, B, C & H: Gettyone Stone, D: Corbis/WildCountry, F: Tony Stone, G: Bluewater, **p. 11** A, D & G: Scottish Viewpoint/Paul Tompkins, B: FLPA/W Broadhurst, C: Scottish Viewpoint/Leo-Clarke, E: Scottish Viewpoint/Wattie Cheung, F: Scottish Viewpoint/Visit Scotland; **p. 12** A & B: David Tarn, C & E: Scottish Viewpoint/Paul Tomkins, D: Scottish Viewpoint/Marius Alexander; **p. 13** B: Scottish Viewpoint/Tom Kidd, C: Scottish Viewpoint/Ken Patterson, D: Corbis/Peter Turnley; **p. 17** C: University of Dundee; **p. 19** C: Scottish Viewpoint/Colin McPherson, D: Scottish Viewpoint/Hubert Ragout, E: Scottish Viewpoint/imagingbody.com, F: Philip Duffy; **p. 20** A, B, C, D & F: Scottish Viewpoint/Paul Tomkins, E: Scottish Viewpoint/Visit Scotland; **p. 21** G: Scottish Viewpoint/Dave Black, H: FLPA/Roger Wilmshurst, I: Scottish Viewpoint/Ken Patterson, J: Scottish Viewpoint/Paul Tomkins; **p. 24** A: Panos Pictures/A. le Garsmeur, B: Panos Pictures/Rob Cousins, C: Robert Harding/Doug Traverso, D: Popperfoto/Reuters/Rafiqur Rahman E: Science Photo Library/Ted Kerasote; **p. 25** F: Woodfall Wild Images/Nigel Hicks, G: Robert Harding/C. Bowman, H: Hutchison Library/Ian Lloyd; **p. 26** B: Flying Colours, E: Hutchison Library/Crispin Hughes; **p. 27** H: Still Pictures/David Drain; **p. 28** A: Panos Pictures/Betty Press, B: Robert Harding/Brian Harrison; **p. 30** A: Panos Pictures/Jon Spaull; **p. 35** A & B: Rob Bowden; **p. 36** D: Rob Bowden; **p. 38** A: Panos Pictures/Jeremy Hartley; **p. 40** A: Science Photo Library/Ted Kerasote, B: Robert Harding Picture Library; **p. 42** A: Robert Harding/Explorer, B: Still Pictures, C: Spectrum Colour Library; **p. 44** A: Corbis, B: Sue Cunningham; **p. 45** C: Stock Market; **p. 46** E & F: Sue Cunningham; **p. 47** G: Science Photo Library/Tom van Sant, Geosphere Project/Planetary Visions; **p. 50** A: Sue Cunningham; **p. 51** C: Sue Cunningham; **p. 52** E: Sue Cunningham, F: Sue Cunningham/Patrick Cunningham; **p. 53** H: Sue Cunningham; **p. 54** J: Oxford Scientific Films/George Bernard; **p. 60** A: Sue Cunningham; **p. 61** C: Sue Cunningham; **p. 63** E: Science Photo Library/NASA; **p. 64** G: Sue Cunningham; **p. 68** A: Still Pictures/Pierre Gleizes, B: World Pictures, C: Spectrum Colour Library/P Thompson; **p. 69** D: Robert Harding Picture Library/C. Martin, E: World Pictures, F: Robert Harding Picture Library/S. Harris; **p. 70** A: Still Pictures/Patrick Bertrand, B: Magnum Photos/Gilles Peress, C: Spectrum Colour Library; **p. 72** A: Robert Harding Picture Library, B: Still Pictures/Klein/Hubert; **p. 74** A: Spectrum Colour Library; **p. 78** A: Woodfall Wild Images/Bob Gibbons; **p. 79** B: Environmental Images/Oliver Waterlow; **p. 80** C: Science Photo Library, D: Still Pictures/J.F.Mutzig, E: Still Pictures/Pierre Gleizes; **p. 81** F: Oxford Scientific Films/Raymond Blythe; **p. 82** A: Robert Harding Picture Library/E. Simanor; **p. 84** Corbis; **p. 88 & 110** C: Eye Ubiquitous/Nick Bonetti, D: Eye Ubiquitous/Chris Fairdough; **p. 89 & 110** E: Robert Harding Picture Library/Nigel Blythe, F: Spectrum Colour Library, G: Robert Harding Picture Library, H: Still Pictures/Harmut Schwarzbach; **p. 91** D: Science Photo Library/Worldsat International & J. Knighton, E: Science Photo Library/Julian Baurn & David Angus; **p. 92** B: Eye Ubiquitous/Paul Thompson; **p. 93** D: Robert Harding Picture Library/Adam Woolfitt; **p. 94** A: Spectrum Colour Library, B: The Art Archive/Musee Guiment Paris/Dagli Orti; **p. 96** B: Robert Harding Picture Library/Tony Waltham, C: Robert Harding Picture Library/Gina Corrigan, D: Picture Works/Ingrid Booz Moreiohn; **p. 97** E: Associated Press/Greg Baker, F: Associated Press/Zhou Wenguang; **p. 99** D: Spectrum Colour Library; **p. 100** *top*: Robert Harding Picture Library/Gavin Hellier, *middle*: Spectrum Colour Library, *bottom*: Corbis/Steve Kaufmal; **p. 101** *top*: Magnum Photos, *middle*: Still Pictures/Francois Suchel; **p. 103** *top*: Rex Features/IWASA, *middle*: Associated Press/David Guttenfelder, *bottom*: Science Photo Library/NASA; **p. 105** D: Robert Harding/Chester Beatty Library, E: James Davis Travel Photography, F: Eye Ubiquitous/Frank Leather; **p. 106** A: Associated Press/Zxinhua; **p. 107** E: Picture Works/Ingrid Booz Morejohn; **p. 108** C: Mitsubishi Electric Europe; **p. 109** E: Spectacular China; **p. 112** A: Still Pictures/Mark Edwards, B, D, F & G: Spectrum Colour Library, C Hutchison Picture Library/Nigel Sitwell, E: World Pictures; **p. 116** A & B: Skyscan; **p. 118** A: World Pictures; **p. 122** D: Rex Features/Nils Jorgensen, E: Associated Press/Findlay Kember, F: Still Pictures/Klaus Andrews; **p. 124** A: Getmapping.com, C: BMW AG; **p. 126** C: Garett Nagle; **p. 127** D: Garett Nagle, E: Chris Honeywell; **p. 128** B & C: BMW AG; **p. 129** D: BMW AG; **p. 132** A: Aviemore Photographic; **p. 134** D: Scottish Viewpoint/Peter Cairns; **p. 137** A: Scottish Viewpoint/Paul Tomkins; **p. 142** B: Science Photo Library/Dr. Jeremy Burgess; **p. 143** D: Still Pictures/Fred Dott, E: Environmental Images/S. Mahoney; **p. 144** A: Science Photo Library/Microfield Scientific Ltd, B: Still Pictures/Roland Birke, C: Oxford Scientific Films/Paul Kay, D: Oxford Scientific Films/Sue Scott, E: Still Pictures/J.P. Sylvestre, F: Woodfall Wild Images/Mark Hamblin, G: Woodfall Wild Images/Tom Campbell, H: Woodfall Wild Images/Bill Coster, I: Science Photo Library/Rudiger Lehnan; **p. 148** A: Axiom/Jonathan Renouf; **p. 149** C: Greenpeace, D: Science Photo Library/Tom McHugh; **p. 150** E: Still Pictures/Klaus Andrews, F: Robert Harding Picture Library, G: Science Photo Library/NASA; **p. 151** H: Still Pictures/Hartmut Schwarzbach, I: Science Photo Library/Simon Fraser, J: Environmental Images/Martin Bond; **p. 152** L: Greenpeace; **p. 153** O: Oxford Scientific Films/Colin Monteath, P: Panos Pictures/Fred Hoogervorst;

Text, Maps and Diagrams

p. 8 A: Philips Foundation Atlas 7th edition / George Philip Ltd; **p. 14** A-D: Philips Foundation Atlas 7th edition / George Philip Ltd; **p. 16** B: The Met. Office; **p. 26** A: Human Development Report 1999 by United Nations Development Program, copyright - 1999 by the United Nations Development Programme. Used by permission of Oxford University Press, Inc., B: DFID *Eliminating World Poverty*, C: World Bank *World Development Report 1999*, D: ActionAid *Fighting Poverty Together*; **p. 27** G: Western Mail & Echo Ltd; **p. 29** C: Human Development Report 2000 by United Nations Development Program, copyright - 2000 by the United Nations Development Programme. Used by permission of Oxford University Press, Inc.; **p. 32** A: World Bank, B: Human Development Report 1999 by United Nations Development Program, copyright - 1999 by the United Nations Development Programme. Used by permission of Oxford University Press, Inc.; **p. 34** A: Human Development Report 1999 by United Nations Development Program, copyright - 1999 by the United Nations Development Programme. Used by permission of Oxford University Press, Inc.; **p. 37** A: Human Development Report 1999 by United Nations Development Program, copyright - 1999 by the United Nations Development Programme. Used by permission of Oxford University Press, Inc., B: Human Development Report 2000 by United Nations Development Program, copyright - 2000 by the United Nations Development Programme. Used by permission of Oxford University Press, Inc.; **p. 40** C: Forestry Stewardship Council A.C.; **p. 48** C: Philips Atlas / George Philip Ltd; **p. 49** A: Attica Interactive 1997, B: Philips Atlas / George Philips Ltd; **p. 95** C: *The Times* (12.10.2000, 05.04.2001), *The Guardian* (03.04.2001, 05.04.2001, 15.05.2001, 13.06.2001), *The Daily Telegraph* (01.12.2000); **p. 99** B: Human Development Report 1998 by United Nations Development Program, copyright - 1998 by the United Nations Development Programme. Used by permission of Oxford University Press, Inc.; **p. 115** F: *The Guardian* (07.1999); **pp. 117, 126 & 133**: Maps reproduced from Ordnance Survey mapping with the permission of the Controller of Her Majesty's Stationery Office, © Crown copyright. All rights reserved. Licence no. 100000230.

Cover photographs by Stone and Corbis/Sandro Vannini

Throughout the book these symbols are used with activities that use literacy, numeracy and ICT skills.

Contents

1 Exploring Scotland   **4**

What is Scotland really like?	5
What do you mean by Scotland?	6
Getting to know Scotland	8
What images do you have of Scotland?	10
What images do people abroad have of Scotland?	11
Where are you in Scotland?	12
What is the weather like?	14
Why does Britain's weather change?	16
What do Scots do for a living?	18
Scotland and tourism	20
Planning a tour of Scotland	22
Review and reflect	23

2 What is development?   **24**

Perceptions of development	25
Development and quality of life	28
Regional variations in development	30
Mapping development	32
Inequalities in development	34
Contrasting lifestyles in Kenya	35
Progress in development	37
Sustainable development	40
Review and reflect	42

3 Investigating Brazil   **44**

What do you know about Brazil?	45
Location, location, location	48
How big is Brazil?	49
What is Brazil like? What are the main differences within the country?	50
What is a developed country?	56
How developed is Brazil?	58
How successful has development been in Brazil?	60
Review and reflect	66

4 France   **68**

The changing economic geography of France	68
What is France's economy like? How is it changing?	70
What changes have occurred in the agricultural industry?	72
What changes have occurred in the manufacturing industry?	74
What is the pattern of tourism in France?	76
What energy resources does France have?	79
France's energy mix – the nuclear power debate	82
International trade	84
Review and reflect	87

5 Comparing countries   **88**

What do we do when we compare countries?	88
Where are China and Japan?	90
China – where do people live and work?	92
China – the physical environment	96
Are there regional differences within China?	98
Are there regional differences within Japan?	100
Japan – the physical environment	102
Trading places?	106
What links do China and Japan have with the UK?	108
Review and reflect	110

6 Tourism – good or bad?   **112**

What is tourism?	112
How important is tourism as an economic activity?	113
How and why is the tourism industry changing?	114
How can tourism be more sustainable?	120
Review and reflect	121

7 Cars on the Internet   **122**

The global car industry	122
The UK car industry	124
Car production in Europe	130
Review and reflect	131

8 Local actions, global effects   **132**

Fieldwork enquiry	133
What conflicts occur between recreational activities?	137
How do people use and misuse rivers?	140
How does water become polluted?	142
'Behold the sea, the teeming sea …'	144
How is the North Sea being polluted?	146
Global effects	148
Review and reflect	154

Glossary   **156**

Index   **159**

Websites On pages where you are asked to go to www.heinemann.co.uk/hotlinks to complete a task or download information, please insert the code **5449P** at the website.

 # Exploring Scotland

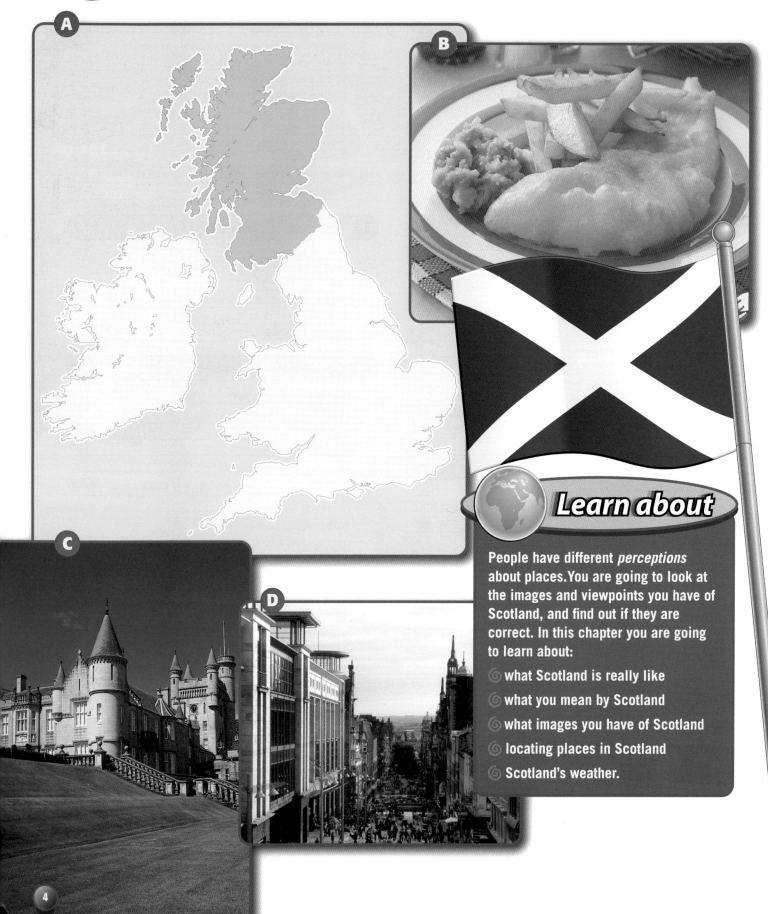

A

B

C

D

Learn about

People have different *perceptions* about places. You are going to look at the images and viewpoints you have of Scotland, and find out if they are correct. In this chapter you are going to learn about:

- what Scotland is really like
- what you mean by Scotland
- what images you have of Scotland
- locating places in Scotland
- Scotland's weather.

What is Scotland really like?

A **Jasbir, aged 11**
66 It's not fair that so many people in Edinburgh are wealthy. 99

B **Kerrie, aged 14**
66 Scotland is a great place, because it's full of old buildings, narrow streets, cathedrals and many attractions. 99

C **Heidi, aged 12**
66 Scottish people are so unhealthy – all those fried meals! 99

D **Asma, aged 13**
66 Robert Burns was born in Alloway, Ayrshire. 99

E **Carl, aged 15**
66 Scotland is a major producer of whisky. 99

F **Amy, aged 14**
66 Scotland is a multi-cultural society. 99

G **Joe, aged 17**
66 Scotland has a great history. 99

Activities

1. Study quotes **A** to **I** about Scotland and decide which are facts and which are opinions. Organise them into a copy of the table below.

Facts	Opinions

2. Choose one fact and one opinion from your list.

   a How did you decide that something was a fact?

   b How did you decide that something was an opinion?

3. Investigate people's viewpoints in your own class or family.

   a How do they compare with the views of people shown here?

   b Why do you think people have different **perceptions** of Scotland?

H **Brett, aged 11**
66 Ben Nevis is Scotland's highest mountain. 99

I **Su-yin, aged 16**
66 Scottish weather is OK – when the rain stops! 99

What do you mean by Scotland?

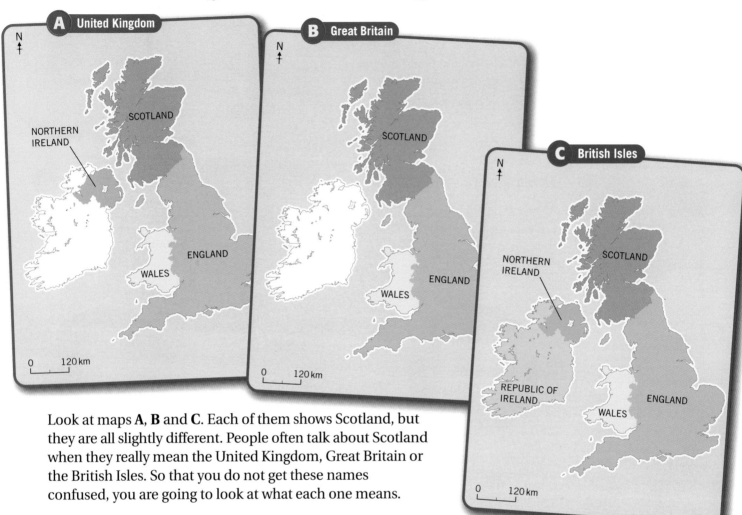

A United Kingdom

N

SCOTLAND

NORTHERN
IRELAND

ENGLAND

WALES

0   120 km

B Great Britain

N

SCOTLAND

ENGLAND

WALES

0   120 km

C British Isles

N

NORTHERN
IRELAND

SCOTLAND

REPUBLIC OF
IRELAND

ENGLAND

WALES

0   120 km

Look at maps **A**, **B** and **C**. Each of them shows Scotland, but they are all slightly different. People often talk about Scotland when they really mean the United Kingdom, Great Britain or the British Isles. So that you do not get these names confused, you are going to look at what each one means.

Activities

1. Draw a Venn diagram, like the one opposite, to show the United Kingdom, Great Britain and the British Isles.

2. In a group, discuss why you think Scotland is part of all three maps **A**, **B** and **C**.

3. Use your Venn diagram and the ideas from your discussion to write a paragraph about Scotland.

4. Complete the sets in the table to show minor places that are part of each whole place. Use an atlas showing the British Isles to help you.

Scotland	England	Wales	Northern Ireland	Republic of Ireland
Aberdeen	Newcastle	Cardiff		
Cairngorms	East Anglia	Anglesey		

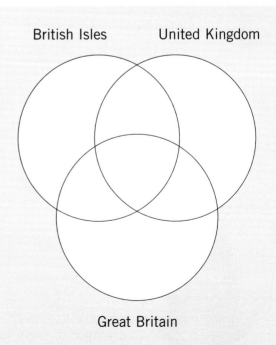

British Isles   United Kingdom

Great Britain

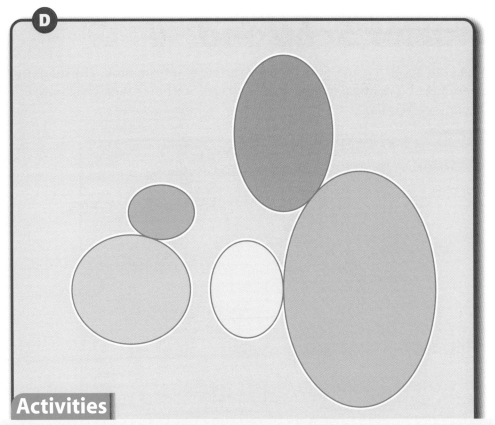

Figure **D** shows a different way of *representing* Scotland and the countries around it. It is a good idea to illustrate something in a different way because it makes you think about what it really shows.

Activities

1. Look at **D**. Find another way to represent Scotland using your own **symbols**.

2. Using an atlas, label your map of Scotland with:

   a five upland areas   **b** five cities
   c five rivers   **d** the place where you live.

   Check the atlas to make sure you use the correct symbols for each of these.

3. **Extension**
   Scotland, the United Kingdom, Great Britain and the British Isles make up parts of Europe and the whole world. Using symbols or a map, show how:
   a Scotland is part of Europe   **b** Scotland is part of the world.

   Try to think creatively and be imaginative in how you represent the connections.

	England	Scotland	Wales	Northern Ireland	Republic of Ireland
Population (millions)	48.5	5	3	1.5	3.5
Area (km²)	130 000	77 000	21 000	13 500	69 000

E Population and area statistics for parts of the British Isles

4. Copy out the table below. Complete it by regrouping the information from table **E**.

	United Kingdom	Great Britain	British Isles
Population (millions)			
Area (km²)			

5. Write five bulleted statements to summarise the differences in population and area between the United Kingdom, Great Britain and the British Isles.

Getting to know Scotland

Using a map is a good way to find out about a place. Maps show a variety of information. The maps on this spread show the physical, human and political make-up of Scotland. See how much you know, or can find out, about your own country – Scotland.

A Physical map of Scotland

Key
- water features
- lowlands
- uplands
- ~ rivers
- ~ roads

Activity

1. Give a blank map of Scotland the title 'Selected physical features of Scotland'. Use map **A** to help you mark the physical features listed below on your map. Make a key to show which type of feature each one is.
   - **Islands:** Arran, Mull, Orkney, Shetland, Skye, Western Isles
   - **Upland areas:** Grampian Mountains, North West Highlands, Southern Uplands
   - **Mountains:** Ben Cruachan, Ben Lomond, Ben Macdui, Ben Nevis
   - **Water features:** Atlantic Ocean, Firth of Clyde, Firth of Forth, Firth of Tay, The Minch, Moray Firth, North Sea, Pentland Firth, Solway Firth
   - **Rivers:** Clyde, Dee, Forth, Nith, Spey, Tay, Tweed

Where is your town?

B | **Main Scottish settlements**

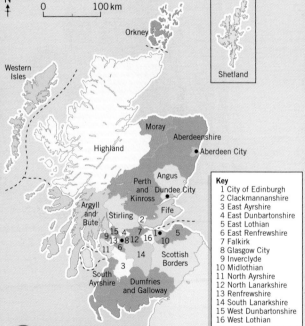

Key
1 City of Edinburgh
2 Clackmannanshire
3 East Ayrshire
4 East Dunbartonshire
5 East Lothian
6 East Renfrewshire
7 Falkirk
8 Glasgow City
9 Inverclyde
10 Midlothian
11 North Ayrshire
12 North Lanarkshire
13 Renfrewshire
14 South Lanarkshire
15 West Dunbartonshire
16 West Lothian

C | **Political map of Scotland: local authorities**

Activity

2 Give a second blank map of Scotland the title 'Selected human features of Scotland'. Use map **B** to mark these settlements on your map: Aberdeen, Aviemore, Ayr, Campbelltown, Clydebank, Dumfries, Dunbar, Dundee, Edinburgh, Elgin, Fort William, Glasgow, Glenrothes, Greenock, Hawick, Inverness, Irvine, Kirkwall, Kilmarnock, Kyle of Lochalsh, Lerwick, Mallaig, Oban, Portree, Paisley, Peterhead, Perth, Stirling, Stornoway, Stranraer, Thurso, Ullapool, Wick.

Map **C** shows the political map of Scotland. The coloured areas represent the local councils who provide many of the day-to-day services, such as libraries, refuse collection and social work, for the people of Scotland.

Activity

3 **a** Use map **C** to find and name your local council.
  b Describe the location of your council.
  c Which council is the largest in Scotland? Can you think why this might be?
  d How many local councils are there in Scotland?
  e What other political body has an impact on the whole of Scotland?
  f Find out more about local government in Scotland and the Scottish Parliament by following the links on www.heinemann.co.uk/hotlinks **ICT**

What images do you have of Scotland?

Activities

1 Look at images **A** to **I**. Decide which of these categories each image belongs to:

⑥ definitely in Scotland   ⑥ unlikely to be in Scotland

⑥ probably in Scotland   ⑥ definitely not in Scotland.

2 Share your ideas with the rest of your group. Be prepared to *justify* your ideas.

3 Choose one of the images that you decided were 'definitely in Scotland'. Answer these questions about your chosen image.

a Why is it Scotland?   **d** Who would live or visit there?

b Where could it be in Scotland?   **e** Will the place always be like it is now?

c What impressions does the image give you?

4 Is the image you chose an accurate reflection of what Scotland is like?

What images do people abroad have of Scotland?

Now that you have worked out your image of Scotland, you are going to explore what people abroad think of the country. The images on this page are taken from a variety of sources that promote Scotland and the Scottish people to people abroad. They show what ideas people around the world have of Scotland today. How correct are these images? When you look at other countries in the world, remember that if people abroad can have misleading images of Scotland, Scottish people can also have misleading images of other countries and peoples.

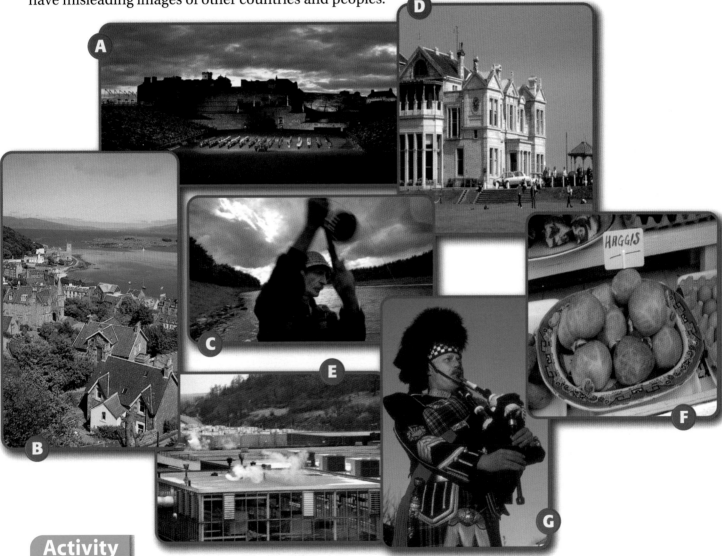

Activity

1 **a** Working in pairs, look at all the images on this page. Then make a copy of the table below.

Accurate images	False images

   b Decide if each image gives an accurate or false view of Scotland today.
      Write the letter in the correct column.

Where are you in Scotland?

To identify places, you need to think about their characteristics and features. Every place is unique, from the largest city to the smallest village. The place where you live has its own identity.

Activities

1 Where am I?

This place:

- has a castle on a rock
- is known as the 'Athens of the north'
- is the home of the Scottish Parliament
- has a famous street called the Royal Mile
- is the capital city of Scotland
- has two football teams – Hearts and Hibs
- is known as 'Auld Reekie'
- has a district called the 'New Town' even though it is several hundred years old
- holds an Arts Festival and Military Tattoo every year.

A

C

D

B

E

2 Each member of a group in turn thinks of a place. The rest of the group must try to find out the identity of the place by asking questions. They must guess the place within ten questions. The help box gives you suggestions of how to ask questions.

Research activity

3 Investigate the images that other Scottish cities and towns present of themselves on the Internet.

help!

There are many different ways of finding out information. To find out more about a place, you could start your questions with the words:

- What ...?
- Where ...?
- When ...?
- Why ...?
- Who ...?

Is this where you live?

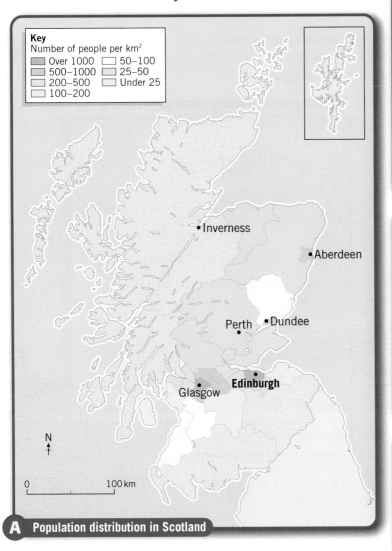

Key
Number of people per km²
- Over 1000
- 500–1000
- 200–500
- 100–200
- 50–100
- 25–50
- Under 25

Inverness

Aberdeen

Perth • Dundee

Edinburgh
Glasgow

N

0   100 km

A Population distribution in Scotland

B Inverness

C Stornoway

D Dunoon

Activities

1. Look at map **A**. Write a short note to describe the following:
   a the places where many people live
   b the places where few people live.

2. Explain why people in Scotland live in some parts and not in others.

3. **Research activity** (ICT)

   Produce a short report on the settlement you live in. Look up the Gazetteer for Scotland website by following the links on www.heinemann.co.uk/hotlinks. Gather information about the following:

   a Settlement name

   b Settlement type (village, town or city)

   c Settlement location (where is it in Scotland?)

   d Settlement size (how many square kilometres?)

   e Population (how many people in the settlement?)

   f The jobs people do in your settlement

   g Anything or anyone famous or well known from the settlement.

What is the weather like?

Weather in the British Isles is always changing – it can be rainy, windy, sunny, cold and warm, sometimes all in the same day. These different types of weather make up Britain's mild and moist climate, which is said to be **temperate**.

Activities

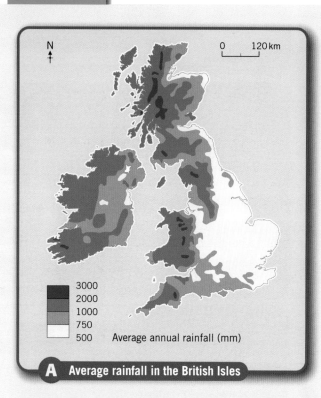

3000
2000
1000
750
500   Average annual rainfall (mm)

A Average rainfall in the British Isles

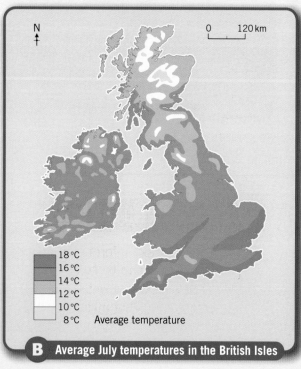

18 °C
16 °C
14 °C
12 °C
10 °C
8 °C   Average temperature

B Average July temperatures in the British Isles

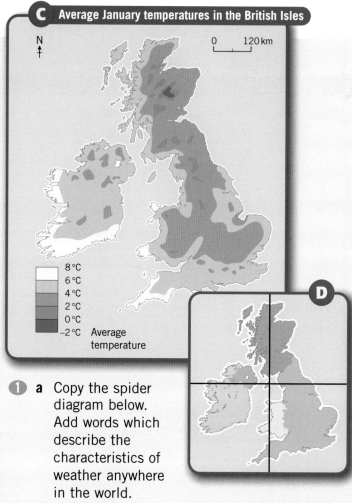

C Average January temperatures in the British Isles

8 °C
6 °C
4 °C
2 °C
0 °C
−2 °C   Average temperature

D

1 a Copy the spider diagram below. Add words which describe the characteristics of weather anywhere in the world.

   b Underline or colour-code words which are only true of weather in the British Isles. Discuss your choice with a partner – how did you make the selection?

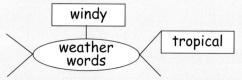

windy

weather words

tropical

2 a In pairs, divide a blank map of the British Isles into four areas, like the one in **D**.

   b For one area, investigate the weather characteristics by using maps **A** to **C**. Work out a way to show the characteristics on your own map.

   c With other pairs, make a full map of the British Isles. Share your information about each area.

Location	Average annual rainfall (mm)	Height of land above sea level (m)
Ben Nevis	3768	1343
Glenmore Lodge	1024	341
Cairn Gorm	2800	1244
Aberdeen	754	65
Eskdalemuir	1456	242
Dunbar	555	23
Goat Fell	2000	874

E Rainfall and height above sea level for some Scottish locations

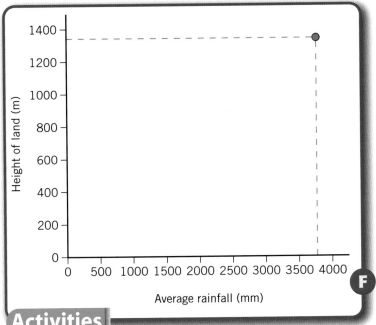

F

How to ...

... draw a scattergraph

1 Label the vertical (*y*) axis with the height of the land (m).

2 Label the horizontal (*x*) axis with the average rainfall (mm).

3 For Ben Nevis:
   - go up the *y* axis to 1343 m
   - go along the *x* axis to 3768 mm
   - plot a point where the two lines meet.

4 Repeat for all the other places on the table.

Activities

3 Use the help box on page 22 to write an account of Scotland's weather in winter and summer.

4 Study the figures on table **E**. Plot the values for each place onto a scattergraph of rainfall and height like the one in **F**. The How to ... box shows you what to do. ①②③

5 Look carefully at your graph. Can you see a relationship between rainfall and the height of the land? ①②③

6 Use your graph to write a summary explaining the relationship between rainfall and the height of the land.

7 **a** Make a copy of the location and weather grid opposite. Use all the information on these pages and an atlas to fill in the remaining spaces on the grid.

   b Can you see any relationships within the grid, for example between relief and other features?

Relief:	Mountainous	Hilly	Flat
Rainfall			
Population			
Other features, e.g. roads			

Getting Technical ▼

You will find more information about weather in Scotland by going to the Meteorological Office website using heinemann.co.uk/hotlinks

Why does Britain's weather change?

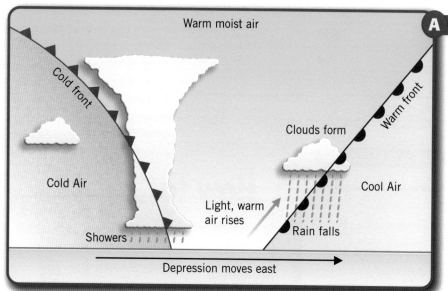

A A cross-section through a depression

Warm moist air

Cold front

Clouds form

Warm front

Cold Air

Cool Air

Light, warm air rises

Rain falls

Showers

Depression moves east

Britain's weather is influenced by two types of **weather systems**:

◎ **anticyclones** (high pressure) bring settled weather – hot in summer, cold in winter

◎ **depressions** (low pressure) bring changeable weather – often rain, cloud and wind.

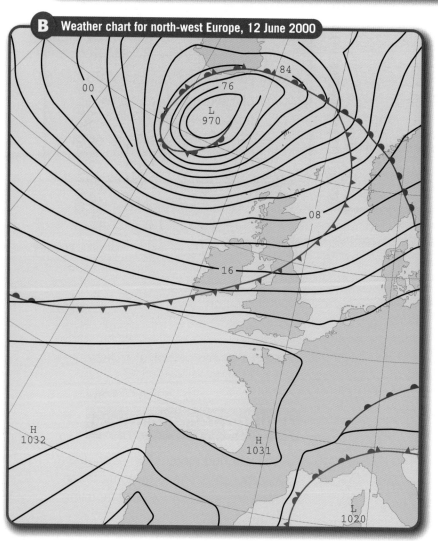

B Weather chart for north-west Europe, 12 June 2000

00

84

76

L 970

08

16

H 1032

H 1031

L 1020

Depressions form over the Atlantic Ocean and move from west to east towards the British Isles. The low pressure draws in warm, moist air from the south and cold air from the north. The warm and cold air masses do not mix. Where they meet, the boundary between them is called a **front**.

Most depressions take one to three days to cross the British Isles, and they bring with them one or more fronts. Figure **A** shows what happens to the weather near a front:

◎ warm air is lighter, so it is forced over the cold air mass

◎ as the warm air rises, it cools down. Moisture condenses into clouds which often bring rain

◎ air is sucked into the low-pressure system, causing winds which blow in an anti-clockwise direction.

Map **B** is a **synoptic chart** for north-west Europe on 12 June 2000. It shows a depression south of Iceland (970 mb) and an anticyclone south-west of the British Isles (1032 mb).

C Satellite image of north-west Europe, 12 June 2000

Activities

1. Read the text and make a list of the characteristics of a depression. Use these headings to help you:
   - pressure
   - wind
   - rainfall.

2. **a** Study map **B**. Make a tracing of the fronts, the area of low pressure and high pressure around the British Isles. Then put your tracing over the satellite image **C** and shade on the area of cloud.
   b Add labels to your tracing to help describe and explain the weather over the British Isles. Use your list from question **1** to help you.

3. Look carefully at all the information you have gathered from questions **1** and **2**.
   a What do you expect would have happened to the weather over the British Isles between 12 and 14 June 2000?
   b Give reasons for your choice of answer.

4. Look out of the classroom window and describe the weather for today.

What do Scots do for a living?

Like people all over the world, people in Scotland have to work for a living. The kinds of jobs people do have changed over time, but they fall into one of three main categories:

⚬ Primary industry: fishing, farming, forestry and mining

⚬ Secondary industry: manufacturing (making things)

⚬ Tertiary or service industries: shops, banks, hotels, cinemas.

Table **A** and bar chart **B** show the changes in employment in the UK between 1980 and 2000. Figures for Scotland would show the same trend.

	1980	1990	2000
Tertiary	16 927	20 286	22 432
Secondary	6 803	5 202	4 236
Primary	634	643	512

A Employment types in the UK, 1980–2000

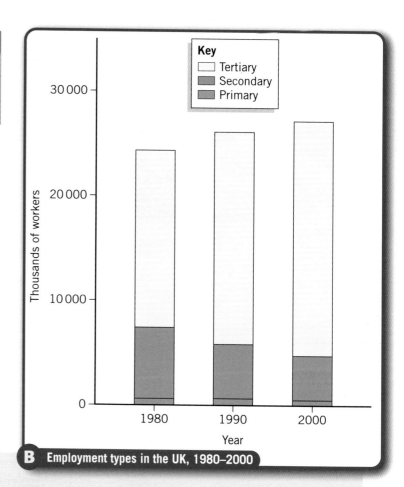

B Employment types in the UK, 1980–2000

Activity

① Look at table **A**.

a Describe what has happened to the number of people employed in primary, secondary and tertiary industries between 1980 and 2000.

b What has happened to the total number of workers between 1980 and 2000?

c Why do so few people in the UK work in primary industries?

d Why has secondary industry declined?

e Why has tertiary industry attracted so many workers?

f What do you think will happen to these figures by 2010?

What comes after tertiary jobs?

Knowledge-based industries will provide the job opportunities of the future. These are called **quaternary industries** and include call centre help lines and hi-tech manufacturing for the computer industry. For example, the European headquarters of computer company Compaq are in Erskine, Scotland. Are these the 'new jobs'?

Why is Scotland first choice for call centres?

The companies below have all set up call centres in Scotland.

Morgan Stanley Dean Witter

'Scotland's wealth of resources was the decisive factor.'

Amelia Fawcett, Chief Admin Officer

Lunn Poly

'We chose Scotland because of the highly skilled workforce, as well as its history of welcoming call centre business.'

Vicky Cook, head of Call Centres

BPS Teleperformance

'Nowhere else offered us the winning combination of a skilled, qualified workforce, with the opportunity of generating substantial local business.'

Andrew Slater, General Manager

NFU Mutual Direct

'I am delighted that we've found the people with the skills to deliver an excellent telephone-based service in Glasgow.'

Andrew Young, Managing Director

beCogent Communications

'The encouragement for new business in this country cannot be overstated.'

Jeff Swanson, Director

Glasgow: the call centre of Britain

In the past most people in Glasgow worked in the docks, shipbuilding or heavy engineering. This is not the case today. The city has changed its image and employment structure. It has attracted a range of 'new jobs', and these have helped to give Glasgow a much better image.

F BT Call Centre, Atlantic Quay, Glasgow, Scotland

Activities (ICT)

1. **a** Look up the Scottish Development International website by following the links at www.heinemann.co.uk/hotlinks and click on the 'Why Scotland' page.
   b View the video images and hear the first-hand experiences of business executives operating call centres in Scotland.

2. Find out more information about other 'key sectors' in Scottish industry.

Scotland and tourism

How important is tourism?

Two kinds of people take holidays in Scotland: British people visiting other parts of the country, and people from overseas visiting Britain. What kinds of places come to mind when you think about tourists? Most people think of the seaside resorts, famous buildings, old cities or special areas like national parks. In fact, tourism can be found just about anywhere in Scotland.

Scotland has a rich variety of attractions to suit all ages and interests, ranging from sailing, skiing, hill walking and mountaineering (active holidays where you do some physical activity) to sightseeing, visiting museums and castles, taking bus tours and steam railway trips (passive holidays, where you sit back and enjoy the view). Visitors are important to Scotland and to the Scottish people. They bring badly needed money to the Scottish economy, and they pay the wages of thousands of workers. The images on these pages show some of the wide variety of tourist attractions in Scotland.

A Kelvingrove Museum, Glasgow

B Cycling in Mabie Forest

C Braemar Highland Games

D Dumbarton Castle and rock

E Sailing in the Firth of Clyde

F Pony trekking at Portree, Isle of Skye

Activities

Use the information on these pages and images **A–J** to answer the following questions.

1. Explain the difference between an active and a passive holiday.

2. Construct a table like the one below. Sort images **A–J** into active and passive holidays. Images **A** and **B** have been done for you.

Active	Passive
B – cycling in Mabie Forest	A – Kelvingrove Museum, Glasgow

3. Add four more active and passive tourist attractions to your table.

4. Tourism creates a lot of jobs in Scotland. Make a list of ten jobs that depend on tourism.

5. Working in groups or pairs, use a large blank map of Scotland and an atlas.

   a Plot each of the locations shown in images **A–J**.

   b Beside each location write a short description of the type of holiday, e.g. **Mabie Forest**: cycling.

   c Add another ten tourist locations to your map using information from the Internet. Follow the links on heinemann.co.uk/hotlinks (ICT)

6. Look up the Travel Scotland website by using heinemann.co.uk/hotlinks and search for the link to Attractions. Find the top twenty paying and free visitor attractions in Scotland.

G Wallace monument, Stirling

H Birdwatching in Orkney

I City bus tour, Edinburgh

J The Abbey on the Isle of Iona

Planning a tour of Scotland

A

MEMORANDUM

FROM: *Area Manager*

TO: *Tour operator*

A party of 55 visitors from the United States will be arriving at Glasgow Airport on Monday at 7.00 am to stay for five days.

They want to see at least seven typically Scottish attractions. Please design their trip and get back to me as soon as possible.

Please note that the group can only travel 300 km (180 miles) per day, so timings are very important.

You will also need to think about the weather people might encounter in different parts of Scotland in June. Think carefully about departure times and the routes used – make these clear on your plan.

Good luck!

B

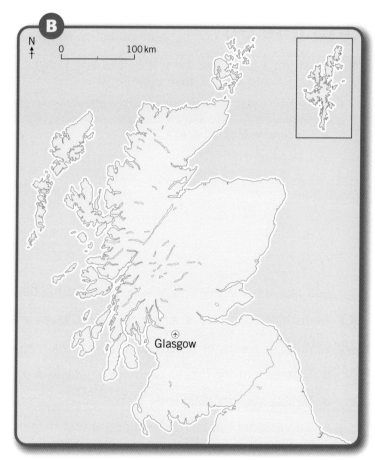

Activities

1 Read the memorandum from Sunshine Tours. In pairs, plan a journey to fulfil all their requirements.

help!

When you do any activity, you naturally follow through a **process of thinking**. This is outlined below. Work through each stage in turn to achieve a structured and accurate piece of work.

- **Cueing** Think about what you want to include in your tour.
- **Acting** Decide on what you are going to do, then design the first draft of your tour.
- **Monitoring** Is your tour meeting all the requirements? Should you add anything or take something out? Design your final piece of work.
- **Verifying** Is your tour complete? Check with your teacher. Share your tour ideas with others.

2 On a map of Scotland, show the destinations, features, routes travelled, distances and timings. Use a different colour for each destination.

3 **Extension**
Use a desktop publishing package to publish an advertising poster or leaflet about your tour. (ICT)

4 **Research activity**
Explore Scotland on the Internet following the links at www.heinemann.co.uk/hotlinks. Choose one region or place you think visitors from the United States might visit on their tour. (ICT)

5 Create a word bank of the words you have learned in this unit about Scotland.

Review and reflect

Odd one out

1 Perceptions	14 Northern Ireland	27 Facts
2 England	15 Republic of Ireland	28 Opinions
3 Images	16 Categories	29 Cueing
4 Weather	17 Reflection	30 Acting
5 United Kingdom	18 Accurate	31 Monitoring
6 Great Britain	19 Justify	32 Verifying
7 British Isles	20 Location	33 Destinations
8 Describe	21 Features	34 Advertise
9 Represent	22 Characteristic	35 Temperate
10 Illustrate	23 Identify	36 Climate
11 Symbol	24 Explore	37 Predict
12 Scotland	25 Promote	38 Actual
13 Wales	26 Places	

Activities

❶ In pairs, look at each set of numbers below. For each set:
  a Find the four words in the list that match the numbers.

  b Try to decide which word is the odd one out.

  c Explain why it is the odd one out and what the other three have in common.

Set A	4	6	35	36
Set B	1	17	27	28
Set C	2	5	12	13
Set D	3	20	24	26
Set E	10	11	16	21

❷ Next, design some other sets to try out on your partner.

❸ Organise all the words on the list into groups. You may have from three to six groups, each with a descriptive heading or title.

❹ **Reflect**

Look back at the images of Scotland that have been used in this chapter.
Discuss with a partner:
  ⓖ which places have been included
  ⓖ which people have been included
  ⓖ which places have been left out
  ⓖ which people have been left out.

Write a short letter to the authors presenting your findings and your point of view.

2 What is development?

Learn about

Development affects us all, but in very different ways. For some it can bring great benefits, such as better jobs or improved health, but for others it brings little change in their day-to-day lives and may even make things worse. In this unit you will explore what development means and you will learn:

- 🌀 what development means to different people
- 🌀 what development means in your local area
- 🌀 how patterns of development vary globally

- 🌀 how different parts of the world are connected by development
- 🌀 how geographers analyse data to understand development
- 🌀 who benefits and who loses as a result of development
- 🌀 what 'sustainable development' means
- 🌀 what governments and others do to help development.

Perceptions of development

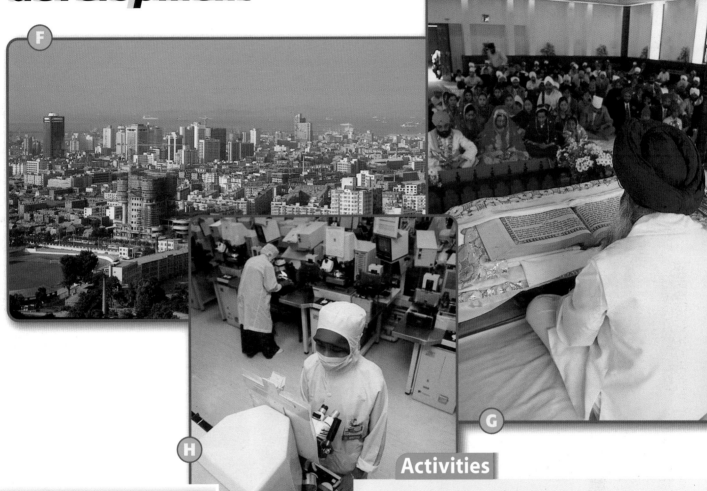

Getting Technical ▾

⑤ **Perception:** the way we experience and interpret (perceive) the world around us. If someone smiles, your perception might be that they are happy. Perception is important to geographers because different people can perceive the same place or event in different ways.

⑤ **MEDCs** (More Economically Developed Countries): wealthy and industrialised nations. They include those from North America and Western Europe and Australia, New Zealand and Japan. They are also known as *Industrialised Countries*, *Developed Countries*, *The North* or *The First World*.

⑤ **LEDCs** (Less Economically Developed Countries): usually poorer and more agricultural nations. Many of these countries are in Central and South America, Africa and Asia. They are also known as *Developing Countries*, *The South* or *The Third World*.

Activities

Discussion activity

1. Working in pairs, study the photographs on these pages.

   a. Decide which images represent 'more developed' places (MEDCs) and which represent 'less developed' places (LEDCs). Write down the reasons behind your decisions.

   b. For each photograph, try to agree on at least two things it tells you about development. Try not to repeat your ideas.

2. Compare your ideas with those of other pairs Make a note of any differences or similarities and discuss your differing perceptions.

3. Using your responses to **1** and **2**, work as a class to try to write a definition of development. Begin with '*Development is ...*'.

4. Start a word bank for this unit with the key words you have used so far. 📖

People think about development in many different ways. Their viewpoints will depend on their own situations and experiences of development. Think about these differing definitions and views of development.

The real wealth of a nation is its people. And the purpose of development is to create an environment for people to enjoy long, healthy and creative lives.

 A United Nations Development Programme (from *Human Development Report*, 1999)

We shall refocus our international development efforts to eliminate poverty. We shall support policies which create sustainable livelihoods for poor people, promote human development and conserve the environment.

Clare Short MP

 B UK Department For International Development (from *Eliminating World Poverty* – Summary, 1997)

Raising incomes is only one among many development objectives. Improving quality of life involves better health services and educational opportunities, greater participation in public life, a clean environment, equity and more.

C World Bank (from *World Development Report*, 1999)

Poverty and the denial of basic needs (such as education, information and security) is a violation of fundamental human rights. The causes of poverty are very much rooted in the unjust distribution of resources. Eradicating poverty without understanding inequality will not yield lasting solutions.

 D ActionAid (from *Fighting Poverty Together: ActionAid's Strategy 1999–2003*)

Development for me is being able to educate my children and keep them healthy so that they have greater opportunities to earn money and have a better life than me.

 E Fisherman, Lake Victoria, Uganda, 1999

Activities

1 a Look at opinions **A** to **E** above. In a group, pick out the key words used to describe development. Write them in a grid like the one here, recording the key word, and the definitions it appears in. The first one has been done for you.

Key word	Definitions	Frequency
Poverty	B, D	3

b Read again the definition of development your class wrote for activity **3** on page 25. Calling this definition **F**, add its key words to your table.

c Now fill in the frequency of each key word you have identified.

2 a Working in a pair or small group, use the five most frequent key words to help write your own definition of development. Compare your definition with those of other groups; have your ideas changed?

b If your views have changed from classroom definition **F**, discuss what might have caused the changes. What does this tell you about definitions and views of development?

3 Add any new words to your word bank for this unit.

4

Extension

Write an acrostic poem like the one here to show what you understand by the word DEVELOPMENT.

D.............................
E.............................
V.............................

Development is not just about global changes and the well-being of whole countries – it involves your own neighbourhood too. In some cases development can happen indirectly through connections between where you live and far-off places. Sometimes development can affect your neighbourhood more directly – for example, there may be plans to build a new road or to close a nearby mine or factory. The newspaper cuttings in **G** are about the development of wind farms in Mid Wales.

£11m wind farm project breezes in

The start of a £11m wind farm project in Mid Wales will provide power for 7000 homes. The managing director of National Wind Power said: 'It will mean a further input of work to the local community and at the same time make a large and positive contribution to the environment.'

Blowing away wind farm myths

… electricity made using coal contributes to global warming and to acid rain, which continues to cause widespread damage throughout Wales. Wind energy, on the other hand, is pollution-free.

Mind blowing

A good night's sleep is just a dream for inhabitants of a once delightful rural Welsh village. The constant drone of twenty new turbines is driving them to distraction. Windmills, they say, have ruined their lives.

Plea for balance in wind farm debate

Wind farms are generally highly visible, and they are sometimes more noisy than they should be. But they are the most energy-efficient of all the electricity generating technologies.

❝ Wind farm power is unreliable. Wind farms with their tiny and unreliable power production can never replace power stations. ❞

Turbine energy is just hot air

… each windmill, put up at a cost of £500 000, will produce no more than 0.00035 per cent of the total UK power requirement.

Four giant turbines at Wales's first commercial wind farm were wrecked when gale force winds ripped across the Welsh hilltop site.

'These awful things could destroy the beauty and quietness of the Welsh countryside when it's covered in these dreadful propellors.'

'Our house is unsellable.'

F Wind farms in Wales

Rhyd-y-Groes• •Trysglwyn
Llyn Alaw•

CAT• •Cemmaes
M. Gorddu• •Carno
•Rheidol •Llandinam
Llangwyryfon• Bryn Titli

Dyffryn Brodyn•
•Parc Cynog
•Taff-Ely

N↑

0 ___ 50 km

G Views on wind farm development taken from the *Western Mail*

H A wind farm at Llandinam, Wales

Activities

❶ Draw two spider diagrams, one to show who will benefit from this wind farm development (the winners) and one to show who will suffer (the losers). Work with a partner or in a small group to add as many connections to the diagrams as you can think of.

❷ Colour code your diagrams in two colours to show who is affected directly and who is more indirectly affected. Remember to add a key.

❸ Using local newspapers or the Internet, research development projects in your own community. Make a list of what the main issues are and repeat activities **1** and **2**. If there are several issues, divide into groups and take one each.

❹ Are there similarities and differences between your local development issues and the development issues in Mid Wales?

Development and quality of life

A Village on Lake Volta, Ghana

B Rush hour on London Bridge

The quality of life enjoyed by individuals depends greatly on whether they live in a more or less developed country. In the UK, for example, a child born today can expect to live for around 77 years, to attend school and to have enough food to eat. But a child born today in Kenya can expect to live to just 52, has only a 68 per cent chance of completing primary school and a 59 per cent chance of regularly getting enough food to eat. People living in more developed countries generally enjoy a better quality of life than people in less developed countries, as shown in table **C**.

Getting Technical ▼

Ⓖ **Standard of living** is used to describe the economic well-being of people. Those with greater wealth are assumed to have a higher standard of living than those with less money. Using this measure, a higher standard of living is achieved by economic growth.

Ⓖ **Quality of life** considers the way in which people live their daily lives, not just how poor or wealthy they are. Do they have enough to eat? Can they afford to educate their children? Do they have shelter at night? These types of questions are asked in order to measure quality of life.

Region of the world	Life expectancy (years)	Under-five mortality rate (per thousand)	Adult literacy rate (%) (US $)	GNP per capita
Sub-Saharan Africa	49	172	58.5	530
Arab States	66	72	59.7	2 200
East Asia	70	46	83.4	1 140
South-East Asia	66	57	88.2	1 130
South Asia	63	106	54.3	490
Latin America and the Caribbean	69	39	87.7	3 830
Eastern Europe and former USSR	69	33	98.6	2 100
Industrialised countries	76	14	97.4	20 900
World	67	84	78.8	4 910

Data taken from UNDP Human Development Report 2000

C Key variations in quality of life by region, 1998

Activities

1. Study photographs **A** and **B** carefully and locate them using an atlas.

2. Draw a Development Compass Rose (DCR) as shown in **D** in the centre of a large sheet of paper.

3. Using the DCR, work in pairs to analyse the two photographs and record your ideas on your sheet of paper. Look for clues that show what types of changes might be happening and who is making the decisions. Are the changes Natural, Economic or Social? Remember that they could be a combination of these.

4. Compare your analysis of the two photographs. Look for issues and questions that are (i) similar and (ii) different. Copy your answers into a table like the one below.

	Similarities	Differences
Natural – environment		
Economic		
Social		
Who Decides? Political		

Extension

Using your work on these two photos, think what a typical day might be like for people living in the locations shown in **A** and **B**. Write a diary entry for someone in each location.

help!

- You may want to use a separate sheet for each photograph, or a different colour pen to show the differences.
- Remember that some of the issues might apply to both photographs.

D Development Compass Rose

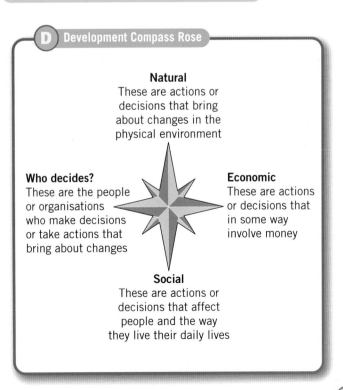

Natural
These are actions or decisions that bring about changes in the physical environment

Who decides?
These are the people or organisations who make decisions or take actions that bring about changes

Economic
These are actions or decisions that in some way involve money

Social
These are actions or decisions that affect people and the way they live their daily lives

Regional variations in development

A Rio de Janeiro, Brazil

Differences in quality of life can also be found *within* countries – people in more and less developed countries can sometimes share a similar quality of life. For example, homeless people living in the UK may have much in common with people in less developed countries. Similarly, wealthy business owners or managers living in Kenya may enjoy a quality of life as good as that of people living in more developed countries, or even better. Geographers call these differences **inequalities** and, as you have seen, they can be studied at any scale from global to local.

Activities

1 Look at photograph **A** and discuss the inequalities that people living here might experience.

2 List the inequalities that can be seen in your own community. Find or take a photograph and annotate it to show these.

3 Using your ideas from questions **1** and **2**, brainstorm what might cause such inequalities. Draw a spider diagram to record your thoughts. Start your diagram with 'Causes of Inequality' in the centre box.

4 Good geographers should look for linkages between different causes, as well as for individual causes. Try to make some linkages in your spider diagram. For example, lack of education often makes it harder to find employment, so 'poor education' and 'unemployment' could be linked by an arrow.

5 Twenty-two per cent of the world's population live on less than US $1 (about 65p) per day. Think about what you could buy with this money. Make a poster to educate others in your school about poverty.

help!

Not all of your ideas are necessarily linked. Others could have several links or be linked in both directions. Think carefully before you mark on the linkages.

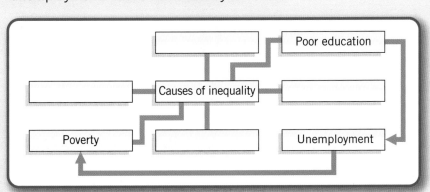

Getting Technical ▼

ⓖ **Gross National Product (GNP):** The value of the goods and services produced by a country and the income it earns from overseas. This is measured in US dollars (US $) and is often divided by the population to produce a measure called *GNP per capita*.

ⓖ **Human Development Index (HDI):** The HDI is used by the United Nations Development Programme (UNDP) to measure development. It is worked out by combining three different indicators: life expectancy, education levels, and income per person. The HDI has a value between 0 and 1 – a higher value means a higher level of human development.

Mapping development

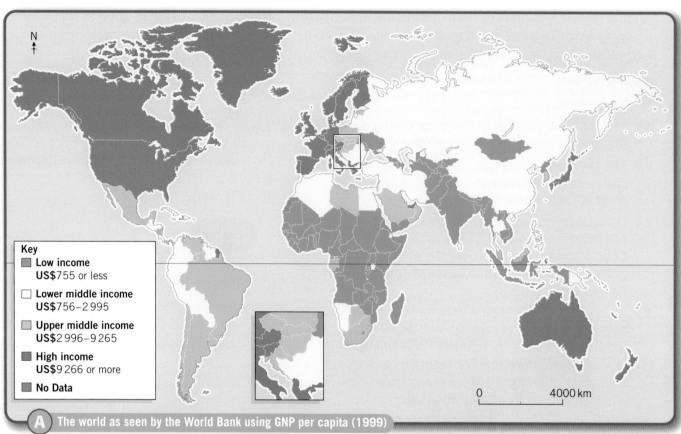

Key

- ■ **Low income**
  US$755 or less
- □ **Lower middle income**
  US$756–2 995
- ■ **Upper middle income**
  US$2 996–9 265
- ■ **High income**
  US$9 266 or more
- ■ **No Data**

0   4000 km

A The world as seen by the World Bank using GNP per capita (1999)

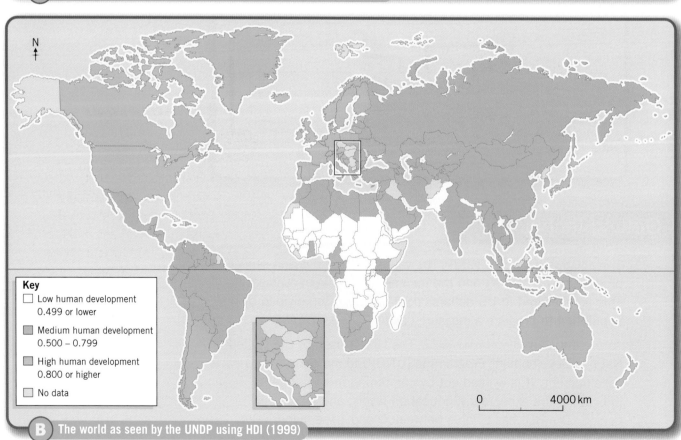

Key

- □ Low human development
  0.499 or lower
- ■ Medium human development
  0.500 – 0.799
- ■ High human development
  0.800 or higher
- □ No data

0   4000 km

B The world as seen by the UNDP using HDI (1999)

Different aspects of development in any one place can be measured using **development indicators**. Many different indicators can be used – so the pattern of development varies, depending on which indicator is chosen.

The World Bank measures development using Gross National Product (GNP) per capita. It uses this measure to divide the world into four different groups of countries: low income, lower-middle income, upper-middle income and high income. According to this method, Luxembourg was the most developed country and Ethiopia the least developed in 1999. Map **A** on page 32 shows how the World Bank views the world.

The United Nations Development Programme (UNDP) uses the Human Development Index (HDI) to measure development. Using the HDI, the UNDP divides the world into three groups of countries: low, medium and high human development. By this measure, Norway was the most developed country and Sierra Leone the least developed in 1999. Map **B** shows how the world looks when measured using the HDI.

Activities

1. Use a blank map of the world and an atlas.

   a Find the countries mentioned on this page and mark them on your map.

   b Choose a way to show the World Bank and UNDP methods of measuring development and use it for the countries you have marked.

   c Choose four more countries from map **A** with low income, lower-middle income, upper-middle income and high income and add them to your map using your chosen method.

   d Choose six more countries from map **B** with high, medium or low human development and add them to your map using your chosen method.

2. Write a geographical description of world development using the same terms that are used by the World Bank and UNDP. Include countries or regions as examples. You may use the writing frame below to guide you.

> World Development can be looked at in different ways.
> The World Bank measures development …
>
> By contrast, the United Nations …
>
> Although the two measures are different, they are alike in some interesting ways.
> For example, some countries …
>
> Other countries …
>
> Another similarity I notice is …
>
> However, there are also some important differences.
>
> For example …
>
> To sum up, when we describe world development …

help!

The following websites can be linked to through www.heinemann.co.uk/hotlinks They contain information about the countries of the world and could be a useful starting point for your research.

✪ United Nations Schools site

✪ Social Watch country data

✪ Central Intelligence Agency

✪ Fact Monster Learning Network.

Remember to look for your own useful websites too.

3. Choose one more developed country and one less developed country. Find out as much as you can about your chosen country using the Internet or books. (ICT)

4. Design a poster comparing development in the two countries you have chosen. Make sure you include information about wealth, quality of life, and inequalities. Include any other information that you think is relevant.

5. Add any new key words from pages 25 to 33 to your word bank.

Inequalities in development

The statistics used to measure a country's level of development are averages, so they often hide large variations in the real situation of people living there. Table **A** shows the differences in income between the richest 20 per cent and the poorest 20 per cent of the population in five countries.

Country	Poorest 20 per cent	Richest 20 per cent
Brazil	$578	$18 563
Kenya	$238	$4 347
India	$527	$2 641
UK	$3 963	$38 164
USA	$5 800	$51 705

A Incomes in US dollars (US $) per year

Source: UNDP, 1999

Activities

1. **a** Make a copy of table **B**.

   b Calculate how big the inequality is between the poorest and richest 20 per cent of the population. Write your answer as a ratio figure. The first one has been done for you

Country	Poorest 20 per cent	Richest 20 per cent	Ratio of richest to poorest
Brazil	578	18 563	32:1

B

2. **Extension**

   Use a spreadsheet package to do the calculations in activity **1** and show your results as a graph. Think carefully about how best to present the information. (ICT)

3. Describe what your results from activity **1** show you. For example, which is the most equal country and which has the greatest inequalities? Your work from page 31 might also help you to explain your findings.

4. What have you learned about the value of using averages to measure development?

How to ...

... calculate ratios

1. To calculate the ratio, divide the larger figure by the smaller figure.

2. The result tells you how many times greater the largest figure is than the smaller figure – the ratio.

3. For example with Brazil:
   18 563 ÷ 578 = 32.11 so the richest 20 per cent earn 32 times more than the poorest 20 per cent.

4. When writing the ratio, round your result to the nearest whole number, in this example: 32.

Contrasting lifestyles in Kenya

Case Study: Alice

My name is Alice and I live here in the West Pokot region of Western Kenya with my husband and four children. I have had seven children in total, but three died before they were even five years old – I was very sad. In our community nearly 150 out of every 1000 children born will die before their fifth birthday. I hope to enrol my children in primary school this year, but it is expensive. My brother has ten children, but only three of them go to primary school. We just don't have enough money – we have just a few goats and our land is not good for farming. Last year we earned just US $120 as a family, even with my husband working at a nearby agricultural project.

A

Case Study: Christopher

I'm Christopher and I work for a travel company in Nairobi. We take tourists to see our wonderful wildlife and spectacular scenery. It is a good job and last year I earned US $2 640, which is much more than I could earn back in my village. It is still difficult to support my wife and two children, however, especially as she is not working at the moment. She insists on looking after our younger child. So many children die when they are young, but the clinic we go to is very modern and loses only 24 per 1000 before they are five, so we are hopeful. If I keep my job, I will be able to send both my children to primary school, but if we have any more children it could be difficult to educate them all.

West Pokot
Nairobi
Kenya
AFRICA
0   1000 km   N
C Kenya

B

Activities

1 Carefully read the case studies of Alice and Christopher on page 35. They represent differences in the quality of life in Kenya.

2 Using data from both case studies calculate the average level of:

a income per person (GNP per capita)

b under-five mortality rate (U5MR)

c primary school enrolment.

3 The data has been adjusted so that the values you calculate represent the national average for Kenya in 1997. In reality you would need a full data set to calculate averages like these. Copy out a table like the one below with seven rows. You could use a spreadsheet for this task. Enter your data for Kenya in the first row. (ICT)

How to ...

... calculate averages

To calculate the average of several values:

1 Work out the values for each example (in this case, Alice and Christopher).

2 Add these values together.

3 Divide the total by the number of values (in this case two values – one for each case study).

For example, to work out the average GNP per capita:

US $20 (Alice) + US $660 (Christopher) = US $680

US $680 ÷ 2 = US $340

Remember, their salaries have to be divided by the number of people in the family.

Country	Average income (GNP per capita)	Under-five mortality rate (per 1000 born)	Primary school enrolment (%)
Kenya			

4 Add the other countries from page 34 into your table and use the Social Watch website (through www.heinemann.co.uk/hotlinks) to find the data for those countries. Use the menus on screen to select your data, countries and year. (ICT)

5 If you have not already done so, find the same information for the countries you selected in question **3** on page 33. Add this to your table.

6 Put all seven countries into rank order for each of the development indicators. If you have used a spreadsheet, use the computer to do this. Does the order of countries vary much? (ICT)

7 **Extension**

Using the Social Watch on-line database, make up your own data tables to compare different development issues for the countries in your table. You could also expand your research to include other countries – for example, one from each continent. (ICT)

D Health care is vital for progress in development

Progress in development

In the second half of the twentieth century significant progress was made in world development. For example, life expectancy increased from a global average of 45 years in 1950 to about 67 years at the start of the year 2000. Improvements in health care and higher levels of education have been two of the main developments responsible for this progress. But just as development levels vary between countries and regions, so too does progress in development. Some regions have improved rapidly while other regions show little progress at all. Table **B** shows the progress in development for the world's major regions between 1970 and 1998.

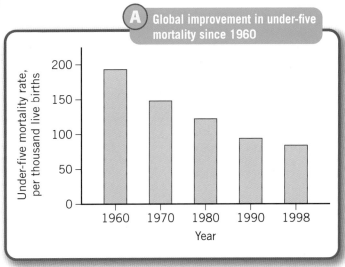

A Global improvement in under-five mortality since 1960

Source: United Nations

Region	Life expectancy (years)		Adult literacy rate (%)		Under-five mortality rate	
	1970	1998	1970	1998	1970	1998
Sub-Saharan Africa	45	49	29	58.5	226	172
Arab States	52	66	31.3	59.7	193	72
East Asia	63	70	81.5	83.4	118	46
South-East Asia	55	66	56.3	88.2	149	57
South Asia	50	63	33.8	54.3	206	106
Latin America and the Caribbean	61	69	72.5	87.7	123	39
Eastern Europe and former USSR	69	69	96.1	98.6	47	33
Industrialised countries	70	76	97	97.4	52	14
World	60	67	n/a	78.8	148	84

B Progress in development between 1970 and 1998

Data taken from UNICEF 1996 and UNDP 2000

Activities

1. Using the data in table **B**, calculate the percentage change in each indicator for the world's major regions. This is a long job, so work in a group or use a spreadsheet package to help you. (1)(2)(3)

2. Look at your results for activity **1**.

   a Which regions have seen the greatest progress and which the least?

   b Which indicator has shown most progress and which the least?

3. Using a blank map of the world, work out a way to show your results from **1** and **2**. Think carefully about the best way to show change.

4. Imagine you are advising on where development efforts should be focused in the future. Using your results from **1** and **2**, write a proposal suggesting what the focus should be and which regions should be targeted as a priority.

Case Study
Who decides?

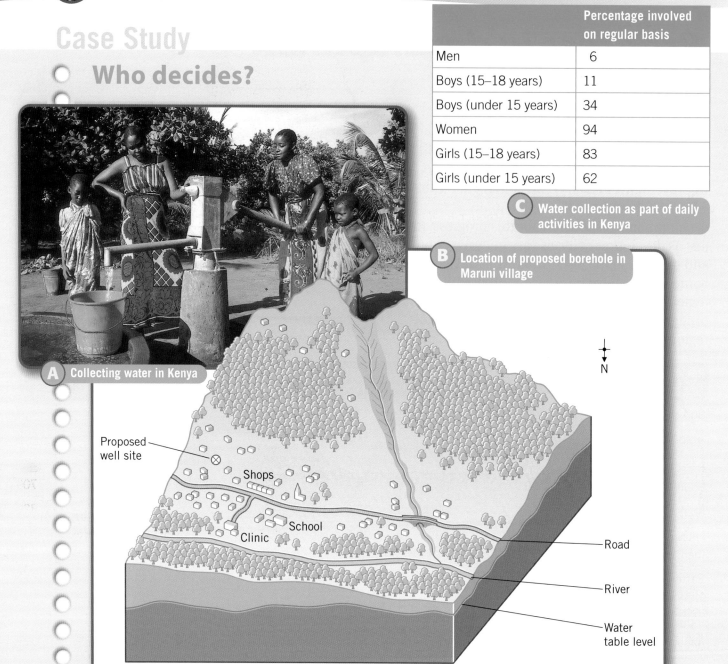

A Collecting water in Kenya

	Percentage involved on regular basis
Men	6
Boys (15–18 years)	11
Boys (under 15 years)	34
Women	94
Girls (15–18 years)	83
Girls (under 15 years)	62

C Water collection as part of daily activities in Kenya

B Location of proposed borehole in Maruni village

N

Proposed well site

Shops

School

Clinic

Road

River

Water table level

Water boost for West Pokot village

Maruni villagers received welcome news today when plans to develop a borehole in their village were announced. Pokot elders finalised plans yesterday with Joseph Lomaria from the regional development authority, who will provide technical assistance, and Philip Saunders, from a UK charity that is funding the project.

Village meetings to discuss water supply problems identified the need for a borehole. At present water is collected from the nearby river, but this is hard work and wastes valuable time. Clean water is found in the rocks under the entire village, but elders decided to drill the borehole in the eastern side of the village where they felt it was most needed.

The local health worker welcomed the announcement. She hopes that a safe water supply would reduce water-related diseases, but stresses the important part played by education in reducing these diseases. She seemed surprised that she had not been consulted on the plans.

The new borehole will be drilled next month and should be in use by the end of the year. There are plans to develop more boreholes if tensions between the Pokot and neighbouring Turkana people subside.

D News extract, 9 October 2000

Collecting water is hard work, but I don't mind it because I get to meet and talk with my friends. We can talk about school. If it took less time to collect water I would just be given another job to do.
(Alice, aged 15)

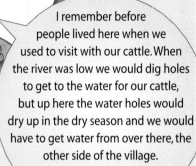

I remember before people lived here when we used to visit with our cattle. When the river was low we would dig holes to get to the water for our cattle, but up here the water holes would dry up in the dry season and we would have to get water from over there, the other side of the village.
(Mzee, old Turkana man from east of village)

I attended the village meetings, but women are not free to speak, we would be told to just keep quiet and let the men make the decisions.
(Perpetua, 34 years old)

I hear what they have said, but do not always agree. When you are young, though, you cannot argue even if you have a better idea.
(Joshua, aged 13)

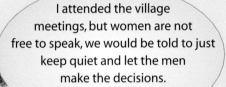
E The views of some local people

Activities

1 a Make a list of the key groups involved in the development project in Maruni village. Be careful to include all those involved in the project and all those who might be affected by it.

b Make a card for each group involved and label it with their group name, for example *Women, Elders*.

c Copy a ladder onto a blank piece of paper. Draw one rung (step) of the ladder for each of the cards you have made.

d Taking each card in turn, arrange them in order of the group's participation and decision-making in the project. Put those who are least involved at the bottom of the ladder and those who are most involved at the top of the ladder.

e Write the groups onto your ladder.

2 Take the cards away and repeat the exercise. This time, put the groups in the order that you think they *should* be in. Remember to justify your order.

3 Compare your new ladder with the first one you recorded. What are the key differences?

4 Repeat the activity for a local development issue in your own community, perhaps one that includes you. Remember to include all those who are involved.

help!

○ Keep moving your cards until you are happy that you have the groups in the order you want.

○ You may think that some groups need to share a rung on the ladder.

Sustainable development

A Clear-cut forestry (where all the trees are cut down) in British Columbia, Canada

B Reforestation in the Sudan, Africa

C FSC

Development does not always bring benefits, especially for the environment. Short-term benefits for some people – jobs and income – often turn into longer-term costs for many people and the environment. For example, the development of the logging and timber industry has led to large-scale deforestation and environmental degradation.

Policies for sustainable development have been introduced by many governments and companies. For example, the Forestry Stewardship Council (see **C**) monitors the number of trees being cut down and ensures that an equal number are planted to provide timber for future generations.

Not all development is sustainable, however. Many development projects continue to threaten the environment today and for future generations. For example, using fossil fuels for energy causes problems such as acid rain and releases large quantities of carbon dioxide (CO_2) – a greenhouse gas responsible for global warming. Fossil fuels are also formed over millions of years, meaning that they cannot be replaced for future generations.

Sustainable Development is development that meets the needs of the present without compromising the ability of future generations to meet their own needs.

D From *Our Common Future* World Commission on Environment and Development, 1987

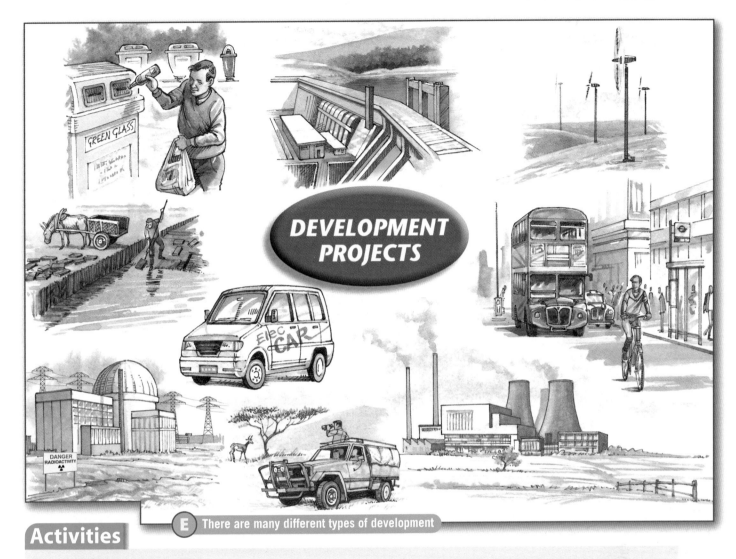

E There are many different types of development

Activities

1 Study the drawings in **E**. Working in a pair or small group, decide which developments you think are sustainable and which are not. Give reasons for your decisions, using evidence to support your argument.

2 Look again at the other examples of development in this unit, including those you have found for your local area. Repeat activity **1** for those.

3 Imagine you are responsible for improving sustainable development. Looking at those projects you have listed as unsustainable, what alternatives might you recommend?

4 Create and carry out a research project to investigate how sustainable your school is.

   a List the sustainable and unsustainable examples that you find.

   b Make a series of recommendations to improve sustainability in your school. Include reasons for your proposed actions and suggest who is responsible for implementing them.

5 Using what you have learned about sustainable development, design a poster to promote the benefits of sustainable development and the actions that individuals can take.

6 **Extension**

Imagine that you can travel forward in time. Write a description of life in the year 2050 if development follows a sustainable path. Then write a description of how life might be if sustainable development is ignored. You could write your description as a short story, a newspaper article, or a poem.

Review and reflect

Development into the twenty-first century

A A sustainable lifestyle in the Kalahari, but little development?

B A Masai herder leaves for the office

C Highly developed Tokyo, but is it sustainable?

As you have learned in this unit, life for most of the world's population improved significantly during the twentieth century. On the whole, people lived longer and were healthier than ever before. However, you have also seen that progress has not been equal and that many people and places still suffer poverty and low standards of living. There are also new concerns about the ability of our planet to support continued progress. People are calling for a rethink about development to make it more sustainable. International targets have been set and development partners, from global institutions to local communities, are working to try to meet those targets. But there is still much to be done. The pace of change remains slow, and it is doubtful that many of the targets will be met on time. So development needs to be a priority for everyone if sustainability is to become a reality in the early part of the twenty-first century.

Activities

1. Look back at the photos in this unit. Working in a pair or small group, select an image that represents one of the key challenges and priorities for development into the twenty-first century.

2. Use the report framework below to plan and write a development report about your chosen image. Include relevant data, words and terms from the unit or from your own research. Remember that you can add your own questions to the framework.

   - What is your chosen development challenge/priority?
   - Why is it a challenge/priority?
   - Where is this challenge/priority most important?
   - What actions need to be taken to meet your challenge/priority?
   - Who should take responsibility and why?
   - What should their target be (what is to be done and by when)?
   - What might get in the way and how might this be resolved?
   - How realistic is it that your challenge/priority will be met on target?
   - Why did you choose that particular issue?

3. Working with your partner or group, prepare a short presentation for the class to explain the key findings of your report. Remember to be prepared to answer any questions they might have.

4. Finally, complete your word bank for this unit with new words and terms from pages 34 to 43.

A São Paulo, Brazil

B Itaipu hydroelectric dam, Brazil

Learn about

This unit is about Brazil. By the time you complete your work on Brazil you will have the skills to make a full investigation of any country in your future studies. You will investigate:

- what it is like to live in Brazil
- the location and scale of the country
- different regions
- whether Brazil is economically developed
- what changes are occurring in the country
- whether these changes have improved the lives of everybody in Brazil.

What do you know about Brazil?

Brazil is a wonderful country – it has everything to offer!

C Ipanema beach, Rio

Brazil is the fifth largest country in the world.

Brazil has the world's ninth largest economy.

There are over 163 million people in Brazil – Argentina, the next most populated South American country, only has 35 million.

Brazil is 8.5 million square kilometres in area. It is by far the largest country in South America.

Brazil has more forest than any other country.

What goes on in these high-rise buildings? Look closely at the photograph to find out whether they are office blocks or flats. Use the Internet to find names of companies which operate there.

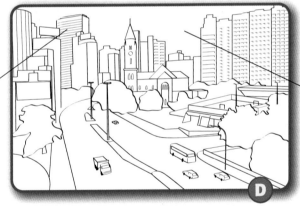

D

What is the temperature? Use the climate maps in an atlas to find the temperatures experienced in Brazil.

Activities

1. Develop a brainstorm diagram to summarise what you already know about Brazil. The photographs opposite may help you to get started.

2. Look at photographs **A**, **B** and **C** in more detail. List all the geographical questions which could help you find out more about each of the pictures.

help!

- This activity is about how to carry out an investigation, so don't worry about the answers to your questions.
- Remember that nearly all geographical questions will include at least one of the words: *What? Where? Why? How? Who?*

3. Suggest how you might start to answer the questions on your list. You could either set your work out in a table, or as labels on a sketch of the photograph (see **D**).

Questions you could ask	Possible way to find an answer
Where is this city located?	Refer to an atlas and find out where it is in Brazil.
How large is this city?	Use a more detailed reference atlas to find out the size of the city and its population.
What language is spoken there? Why?	Use an encyclopedia or textbook to find out about Brazil's past.

Other images of Brazil

E Favela in São Paulo

Brazil fact file

- One per cent of landowners control over half the land in Brazil.
- The richest ten per cent of the population have an average income 78 times greater than the poorest ten per cent.
- Working conditions in some Brazilian factories are terrible.
- Production targets mean that many workers have to work twelve-hour shifts.
- The working week is often very long.
- Seven million Brazilian children are involved in child labour. They often do dangerous work for very low wages.

F Sandy river banks being eroded following deforestation in Para State, Amazonia

    G Satellite image of South America

Key

Andes Mountains

Tropical rainforest

Desert and semi-desert

Grassland and savannah

help!

Try to think about

☻ stresses on the natural environment

☻ economic stresses

☻ social stresses.

Activities

④ Look carefully at photographs **E** and **F**. With a partner, list all the stresses on the environment that you can see in each of the pictures.

⑤ **Extension**

Try to find some more images of Brazil to add to your list of stresses. Look in other textbooks or try the Internet, for example, go to the geography page at the website listed on www.heinemann.co.uk/hotlinks **ICT**

⑥ Look back at the text and photographs on pages 44–47. Draw up a table of the positive and negative images that you associate with Brazil. Add the source of each image.

Positive images of Brazil	Negative images of Brazil
Smart high-rise buildings (source: photo A)	Poor housing (source: photo E)
Successful economy (source: text page 45)	

⑦ This activity is about **locating** photographs **A–C**, **E** and **F**.

a On an outline map of Brazil, show with labels where you think each of the five photographs could have been taken. Give your map a title.

b Give reasons for your choices of location.

c Choose *three* photographs. Write down a more precise title for each of these photographs. Use your answers to **a** and **b** to help you.

⑧ Use your work from activities **4–7** to draft a paragraph to give a visitor to Brazil an introduction to the country.

Location, location, location

When geographers investigate a place, they often look first at its location. Location is usually described by linking the position of that place to the positions of other places. This is called the situation of the place. The starting point for your detailed investigation of Brazil is to ask the enquiry question:

Where is Brazil located?

All the maps on this page show Brazil.

⊚ Map **A** shows Brazil in its global situation.

⊚ Map **B** shows Brazil in its continental situation.

⊚ Map **C** shows São Paulo as a city within a region of Brazil.

The location of any place can be built up within a precise geographical **hierarchy**, like the one in diagram **D**.

B The situation of Brazil within the continent of South America

UK

Atlantic Ocean

Equator 0°

N

Brazil

Brasilia

0   3000 km

A Brazil in its global situation

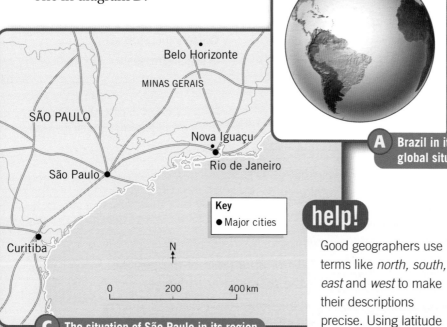

Key
• Major cities

N

0   200   400 km

C The situation of São Paulo in its region

Belo Horizonte

MINAS GERAIS

SÃO PAULO

Nova Iguaçu

Rio de Janeiro

São Paulo

Curitiba

help!

Good geographers use terms like *north*, *south*, *east* and *west* to make their descriptions precise. Using latitude and longitude also helps to locate places exactly.

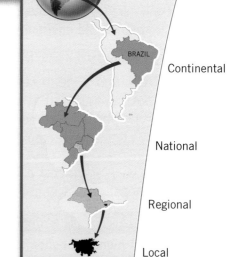

Global

BRAZIL

Continental

National

Regional

Local

D Building up a geographical hierarchy

Activities

① Use maps **A–B**, supported by your atlas, to locate Brazil within the world. Draw a simple sketch map and write two or three sentences to locate Brazil.

② Draw a sketch map to show the situation of Brazil within the continent of South America. Write three sentences summarising what your sketch map shows about the country's situation.

③ Use your atlas to describe an air journey from the UK to Brasilia, the capital of Brazil. 📖 ①②③

⊚ Name the countries and oceans you pass over during your flight, as well as giving the direction you travel and the distances you cover.

⊚ The aircraft needs refuelling at an international airport every 2500 km. There are a number of ways you could do it – safe journey!

How big is Brazil?

If you look at maps **A** and **B**, you will not only see the situation of Brazil but also get a clear idea of the size or scale of the country. This gives a second aspect to the investigation, so you can ask a second enquiry question:

How big is Brazil?

The answer is more useful when the size is given in relation to the size of other countries.

Brazil is a very large country – it is the fifth largest in the world. You can see in table **C** how it compares with some other countries in South America.

A South America

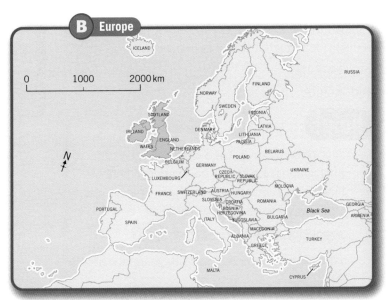

B Europe

0   1000   2000 km

help!

Use the scale line on your map. Measure the distances using a ruler or by marking the edge of a piece of paper.

Country	Area
Argentina	2767
Bolivia	1099
Brazil	8512
Chile	757
Ecuador	272
Paraguay	407
Surinam	164
Uruguay	176
Venezuela	912

C The areas of some countries in South America (thousands of square kilometres)

Activities

1 a Use a map of Brazil to measure the furthest distance from north to south across the country, and from east to west.

b Now do the same for Scotland. Write a sentence or two to compare the sizes of the countries.

c Look at maps **A** and **B**. Work out approximately how many times Scotland could fit into Brazil.

2 Brazil is not the largest country in the world: Use an atlas to work out which countries are larger. Try to put them in order of size.

3 Table **C** only shows *some* of the countries in South America.

a Estimate the size of the missing countries: French Guiana, Guyana, Colombia and Peru.

b List all the countries in South America in order of size, starting with the largest.

What is Brazil like? What are the main differences within the country?

Case Study

Planning a trip to Brazil: can you get the contract?

Activity

1 You work for a company that is trying to plan a field trip to Brazil for school students. You need to convince the school that the students will be well informed about Brazil by the end of their three-week stay.

As you know by now, Brazil is a very large country. It is made up of several regions that have great differences. Some of these differences are shown in these six pages. You must make sure that, by the end of their trip, the students have a clear idea of what Brazil is like overall.

You have been asked to prepare and give a presentation showing the details of your field trip. This should include:

◎ A route map to show where the students will go and how long they will stay in each location

◎ The contrasts in the geography that the students will see in each part of the country that they visit

◎ The reasons for visiting the areas you propose

◎ The best time of the year for the visit, and any precautions that the students should take before starting this trip of a lifetime.

help!

Your presentation could include a display with photographs, itineraries, travel arrangements, timetables, short speeches, diagrams and maps. Useful websites for your research can be found at www.heinemann.co.uk/hotlinks

Briefing notes

Brazil is divided into five regions (see map **B**). These may help you plan your journey, but the students may not be able to visit all five in three weeks. The photographs, diagrams, maps and text on the following pages will give you some idea of each region's character.

What is the South and South-East of Brazil like?

This part of Brazil is divided into two – the South and South-East Regions. Temperatures in the region are tropical: 27–32°C in January, 16°C in July. It is never really uncomfortable by the coast as the sea breezes keep temperatures down, but it can be unpleasantly hot at night. In the South, temperatures are lower. Rainfall totals are high (over 1000 mm), and some areas do not have a dry season. The wettest season is during the summer months – November to April.

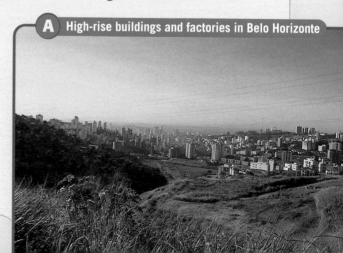

A High-rise buildings and factories in Belo Horizonte

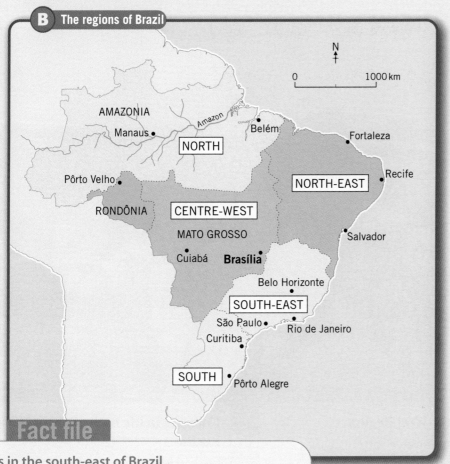

B The regions of Brazil

N

0   1000 km

AMAZONIA

Manaus •

Amazon

• Belém

• Fortaleza

NORTH

Pôrto Velho •

• Recife

NORTH-EAST

RONDÔNIA

CENTRE-WEST

MATO GROSSO

• Salvador

Cuiabá •   **Brasília** •

Belo Horizonte •

SOUTH-EAST

São Paulo •   • Rio de Janeiro

Curitiba •

SOUTH   • Pôrto Alegre

Fact file

Cities in the south-east of Brazil

- ⑥ The cities contain the head offices of many international companies.

- ⑥ The economy grew rapidly between 1960 and 1990 – an 'economic miracle'.

- ⑥ Rapid growth has its costs, with high pollution levels and shortage of proper housing, clean water and rubbish disposal.

In the south-east of Brazil, the Brazilian highlands reach the coast to form an area of steep slopes. Development often only occurs on flat land. This region has the highest mountains of the country. The rest of Brazil is a land of flat horizons.

The south-east has always been important for Brazil. In 1850 the city of São Paulo began to grow because of the rich coffee estates nearby. Today, this is the main industrial region of Brazil. Most of the country's population is concentrated in this region around the three cities of São Paulo, Rio de Janeiro and Belo Horizonte. The area has an important steel industry. The blast furnaces use local iron ore and **charcoal** from the local forests. Agriculture is the most mechanised in the country. Large farms produce coffee, sugar cane and grains for **export**, as well as for food for the Brazilian people.

C Growing sugar cane is highly mechanised

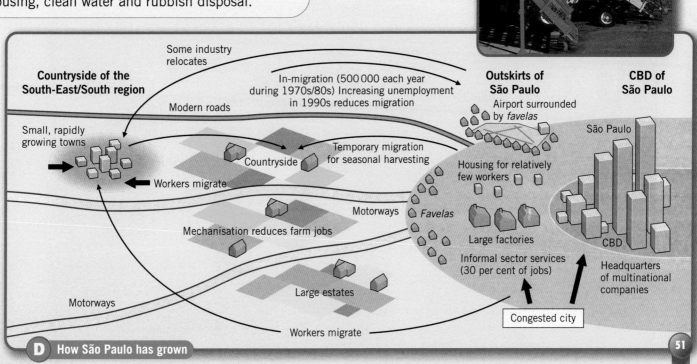

Some industry relocates

Countryside of the South-East/South region

In-migration (500 000 each year during 1970s/80s) Increasing unemployment in 1990s reduces migration

Outskirts of São Paulo

CBD of São Paulo

Modern roads

Airport surrounded by *favelas*

São Paulo

Small, rapidly growing towns

Countryside

Temporary migration for seasonal harvesting

Housing for relatively few workers

Workers migrate

Motorways   ◇ *Favelas*

Mechanisation reduces farm jobs

Large factories

CBD

Informal sector services (30 per cent of jobs)

Headquarters of multinational companies

Motorways

Large estates

Congested city

Workers migrate

D How São Paulo has grown

E Cattle ranching in the Centre-West Region

What is the Centre-West Region of Brazil like?

Inland from the crowded coast of the South-East Region are the high plains of the Mato Grosso. The mountains of the coastal area have merged into a vast **plateau** about 1000 metres high. The monotonous landscape can be seen in photograph **F**. Away from the coast, temperatures become higher and it is less **humid**. Annual rainfall is high (1700 mm) but there is a dry season from May to September. The natural vegetation of this area is **savanna** grassland.

Traditional life in the Centre-West Region

- Poor soils only allowed **extensive ranching** of cattle: fewer than one cow per hectare.

- The few mineral resources were quickly mined.

- Towns were few and far between. They were local market and services centres.

Changes to life in the Centre-West Region

- In 1960 a new capital city, Brasilia, was built.

- People migrated here as farming became more mechanised.

- Soya bean cultivation changed the farming landscape greatly during the late twentieth century.

F Brasilia

What is the North-East Region of Brazil like?

The north-east is much drier than the rest of Brazil, with less than 750 mm of rainfall. However, this rainfall is very unreliable. In the 1970s a terrible **drought** caused out-migration from this poor area. This was one cause of the dramatic growth in many Brazilian cities, especially in the south-east.

The inland part of this region has the least rainfall. The São Francisco River flows through the area. The river often has great changes in water level, and its tributaries run dry during the dry season. In an attempt to supply water throughout the year, the river was dammed at Juàzeiro to form the Sobradinho Reservoir.

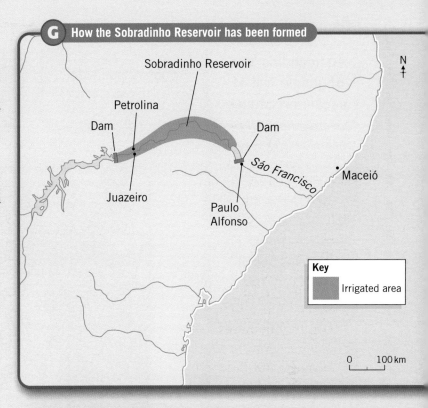

G How the Sobradinho Reservoir has been formed

Sobradinho Reservoir

Petrolina

Dam

Dam

São Francisco

Maceió

Juazeiro

Paulo Alfonso

N

Key

Irrigated area

0   100 km

Brazil invests in alcohol

Sugar cane can be processed to make ethanol (pure alcohol), which may be used as an alternative to petrol. The Brazilian government started a programme in the 1970s to increase ethanol production in the north-east. The aim was to help poor farmers in this underdeveloped area, as well as reducing the need to import oil. This idea may seem good, but sugar cane is grown on large farms, so valuable land is taken away from growing food.

Fact file

The North-East Region of Brazil

◎ It is the largest area of poverty in the Americas.

◎ Urban population is now greater than the rural population because of recent migration to cities.

◎ There is a high density of rural population.

◎ The standard of living is constantly threatened by a lack of basic needs, especially food.

H Farming in the north-east of Brazil

Disaster, famine, disease and drought ravage the land!

Starving mobs ransacked market stalls in a small town in the State of Pernambuco yesterday. A thousand people queued to fill their tins with drinking water. There have been lootings by hungry peasant farmers all over Ceara State. Ninety per cent of all crops have been destroyed by severe drought, which has followed three years of below-average rainfall.

Many people in the area farm very small plots and are unable to save money. Large-scale projects don't seem to make much difference to the plight of the poor.

The Brazilian government declared a state of emergency in the area last night.

I Newsflash from the North-East Region of Brazil, 24 January 1992

What is it like in the North Region?

An unending 'sea' of jungle full of exotic creatures

A landscape laden with moisture

Daily downpours of rain

Massive system that helps stabilise the global climate

Tall trees, both evergreen and broad-leaved

Contains one in thirty of the world's butterflies

Home to 2000 species of fish

One in five of the world's bird species live in one-fiftieth of the Earth's land surface

Hot and wet throughout the year, rotting even people's clothes

Full of stinging and biting creatures

Crawling with huge spiders, many with deadly bites

Home to tribal people who are threatened by 'western ways'

J Amazonia – the final frontier?

 idea Find out more at www.heinemann.co.uk/hotlinks

In the north of Brazil the climate is **equatorial**, with rainfall totals of over 2000 mm. There is no dry season but some months are much wetter than others. The Amazon river flows through this region from west to east. Together with more than 1000 known tributaries, the Amazon makes up the largest river basin area in the world. The landscape is a huge lowland plain, but steep-sided river valleys cause local changes to the soil and vegetation. The Amazon in Brazil has a very gentle **gradient** throughout its 6400 kilometre course, with no land over 250 metres. Large boats can sail a long way up the Amazon, so it is an important transport route.

The **selvas** is the last large area of undeveloped tropical rainforest in the world. For many years the resources of the forest have been seen by the government as a great opportunity to increase the wealth of the country. For centuries people have farmed or gathered natural products like Brazil nuts, cocoa, indigo, vanilla oil and natural rubber from the rainforest. These activities were **sustainable** because they did no long-term damage to the forest environment. More recent developments have often been larger in scale and have had a much greater impact.

There are two main cities in this area: Manaus, the capital of the State of Amazonas, and Belém, which is near the mouth of the river. Both have grown very rapidly since 1990, partly because many of the large-scale agricultural development plans in this area have failed.

K How a rainforest works: an unending 'sea' of jungle full of exotic creatures

What is a developed country?

The students threw a party when they got home from their trip to Brazil. Several of them started talking about what a developed country was. It was a lively party and the discussion became quite heated ...

A developed country is simply a rich country! The rich countries of the world, places like UK or USA, are very developed.
Asma

Surely there is more to development than just money – hasn't happiness got something to do with being a developed person? A developed country is simply a country made up of mainly happy people.
Amy

Development is easy to measure. In developed countries, people on average have a high income. In poor, developing countries people on average have a low income.
Heidi

I'd say a developed country is one in which there is a good education system, a good medical system and a fair system of democratic government.
Kerrie

Whether a country is developed or not must include things like **sustainability** or inequality. I don't feel that Britain is a very developed country – we don't have a sustainable lifestyle. Since the 1980s the gap between the rich and the poor has been getting greater.
Su-yin

I think that the tribal people of the Amazon are among the most developed people in the world. They have lots of leisure time, even though life is short for most of them.
Joe

People are happy when they have money to do what they want – this means that they've probably got a good job which pays well. People in developed countries have got good jobs. Certainly most of them aren't sweating in the fields trying to farm on poor soils with little machinery to help.
Carl

How can a country get developed if it is in debt? No country can be developed if it imports more than it exports.
Malcolm

Developed countries have met the basic needs of all their people, like having enough food, access to water and proper housing.
Jasbir

Activities

1 Read the views of the nine people on the opposite page.

   a Select the person that you agree with most and give a reason for your decision.

   b Repeat the activity for the person you disagree with most.

2 Jasbir gave some examples of basic human needs. What other human needs would you have added to this list?

3 Some people have a rather narrow view of what a country's development is about. Other people feel that the definition is based upon a large number of factors. Divide the views of the nine people into two columns based upon whether you think they have a narrow or broad view of development. The table has been started for you.

Broad view of development	Narrow view of development
Amy	

4 Use a full page to produce a brainstorm diagram showing all the factors that could be used to define development. Use all the views of the people involved in the discussion as well as some of your own ideas.

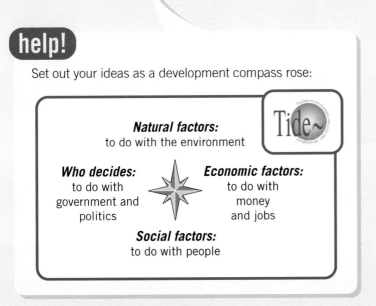

help!

Set out your ideas as a development compass rose:

Natural factors:
to do with the environment

Tide~

Who decides:
to do with government and politics

Economic factors:
to do with money and jobs

Social factors:
to do with people

5 Now it is time to come to a conclusion:

What is a developed country?

Imagine you were at the party. Write down what you would have said after hearing all nine opinions. Try to end up with the best definition of what you think 'a developed country' is.

6 **a** Add your definition to your geography word bank.

   b Look back through pages 44–55 and add any other key words you need to remember.

How developed is Brazil?

There are a number of ways to look at how developed a country is.
One way is to use a map like **A**, which shows world development based
upon Gross National Product.

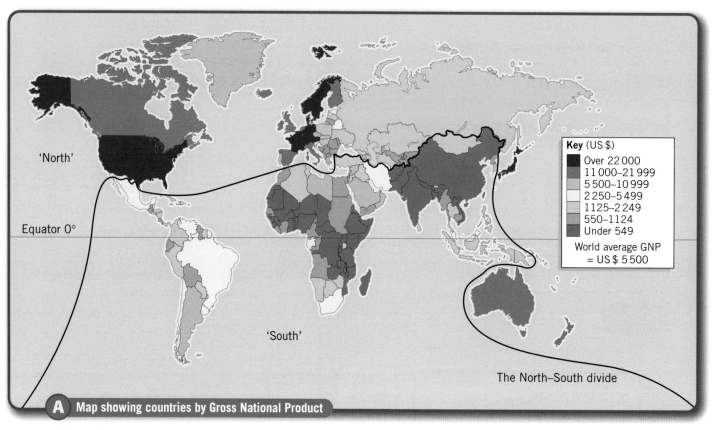

Key (US $)

	Over 22 000
	11 000–21 999
	5 500–10 999
	2 250–5 499
	1 125–2 249
	550–1124
	Under 549

World average GNP
= US $ 5 500

'North'

Equator 0°

'South'

The North–South divide

A Map showing countries by Gross National Product

Although this way of looking at development seems straightforward, many geographers think it is a bit
too simple. **Economic development** is easier to measure than other forms of development. Table **B**
shows some different information for six South American countries and the UK. Some of these figures
may be more important for assessing development than others.

Country	GNP (US $)	Safe water (%)	Adult literacy rate (%)	Life expectancy (years)	IMR (per thousand)	Population growth (%)	Energy consumption (kg oil equivalent)
Argentina	11 728	65	97	73	19	1.4	1 730
Bolivia	2 205	55	87	62	60	2.2	548
Brazil	6 460	72	85	67	33	1.7	1 051
Chile	8 507	85	95	75	10	1.6	1 574
Guyana	760	83	98	64	57	0.8	426
Venezuela	5 706	79	94	73	21	2.4	2 526
UK	20 314	100	99	77	6	0.3	3 863

Data taken from 1980–1998

B Development indicators

Getting Technical ▼

⑥ **Gross National Product (GNP)** – the wealth a country produces, divided by the total population. GNP is measured in US dollars.

⑥ **Safe water** – percentage of people who have access to clean water.

⑥ **Adult literacy rate** – percentage of adults who can read and write.

⑥ **Life expectancy** – the average number of years people can expect to live.

⑥ **Infant mortality rate (IMR)** – the number of babies who die before their first birthday, out of every thousand born.

⑥ **Population growth** – how fast the population is growing, in percentage each year.

⑥ **Energy consumption** – the average energy each person in a country uses, measured in kilograms of oil equivalent.

Activities

① Use map **A** to put these countries in order of economic development. Start with the most developed country.

Brazil   Argentina   Bolivia   Chile   Guyana   Venezuela   UK

② Write a paragraph describing the general pattern of world economic development as shown in map **A**.

③ **a** Look at the development data for seven countries in table **B**. Choose the four indicators which you think give the best overall picture of development. Explain why you have chosen them.

b For each of your four chosen indicators, rank the seven countries in order of development.

c Draw up a final league table based upon the overall average ranks. Highlight the position of Brazil within your league table.

④ In a group, produce a display that compares the development of the seven countries shown in table **B**.

⑤ **Extension**
Use the Internet to research further figures to make your comparison fairer. You could start by going to www.heinemann.co.uk/hotlinks and looking at schools on the website listed. (ICT)

⑥ Write a short paragraph comparing Brazil's development with that of one other country in your league table.

help!

You could use a writing frame to help you extend your description.

The most economically developed continents in the world are …

Countries in these continents have GNPs of about …

The least economically developed continents in the world are …

The other continents include …

help!

In your group display, you could include:

❁ a map showing the location of all the countries

❁ very brief summaries about each country

❁ your four league tables – find a way of showing these graphically and put them around your map. Add the final league table.

The furniture and banana tree come to $6.27 – that means you still owe, er … $999,999,993.73

US BANKS
REPOSSESSIONS Co
(SOUTH AMERICA)

⑦ Explain how cartoon **C** shows the difficulties facing less developed countries.

How successful has development been in Brazil?

A number of developments that have recently occurred in Brazil are discussed in the next five pages. The activities for this section are on page 65. You may be asked to investigate the enquiry question above in groups.

The recent history of Brazil has been full of plans to try to develop the rich resources of the country in order to improve the lives of the Brazilian people. Many of these developments focused on the final frontier – Amazonia.

Transport developments

To make the centre and north of Brazil richer, the government has a vast road-building programme. The dream of the Brazilian government is to build roads westwards until there is a link right across the continent from the Atlantic to the Pacific Ocean. The three main **arterial roads** are:

- the Trans-Amazonian Highway, built in the 1970s

- the Brazilian Road (BR364), which opened up the jungle states of Rondonia and Acre in the mid 1980s

- the Northern Perimetral Highway, which is still under construction.

Feeder roads branch off the main roads to allow farming and settlement of the land. Many roads in Amazonia become impassable in the wet season because they have no proper surface. Paving the roads is very costly and the government has to borrow money to do it.

Roads are one of the main ways to open up the forest. They allow migrants, services and food to be brought into the forest and timber, minerals and farm products to be brought out – building roads is the first stage in destroying the forest.

A The Brazilian Road (BR364) cuts through the rainforest in Amazonia

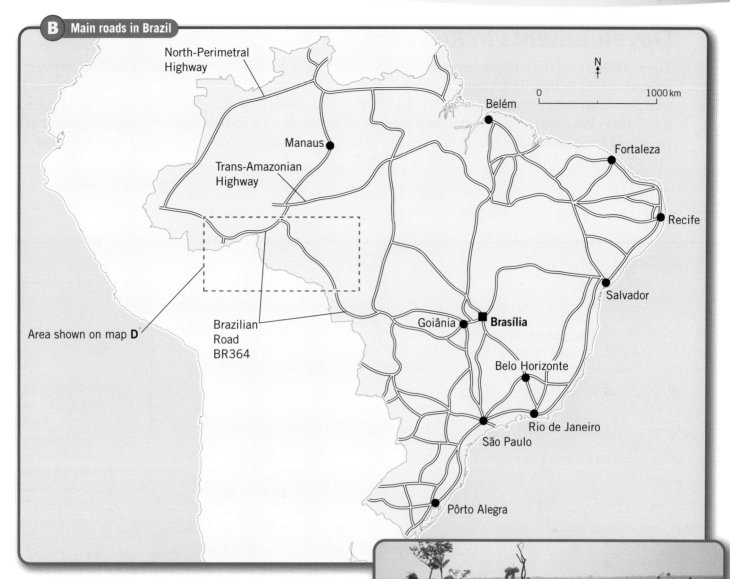

B Main roads in Brazil

North-Perimetral Highway

Trans-Amazonian Highway

Manaus

Belém

Fortaleza

Recife

Salvador

Goiânia   ■ **Brasília**

Belo Horizonte

Rio de Janeiro

São Paulo

Pôrto Alegra

Brazilian Road BR364

Area shown on map **D**

N

0   1000 km

Cattle ranching

Cattle ranching has become one of the main reasons why the rainforest has been destroyed in Amazonia. The ranches are usually very large and many are owned by large, powerful meat-producing companies. The trees are cut down to make room for cattle pasture. There is a great demand for beef in the 'hamburger' culture of the USA, Japan and Europe, and Brazil exports much of the beef it produces. Cattle ranching does provide employment, but one cowboy can manage over 3000 cattle. Unfortunately Amazonia's poor soils do not support good grass growth, so weeds grow which can only be eradicated by **herbicides**. As a result, the land eventually becomes useless. The ranchers abandon the land and wait for land prices to rise before making a massive profit. As more roads are built, more forest timber becomes accessible and more minerals are discovered, so most people expect that land prices will go up.

C During and after the destruction of the rainforest

61

Developments in Rondônia

The Brazilian government encouraged massive migration into Rondônia during the 1980s to try to give poorer farmers some land of their own. First the Porto Velho road (BR364) had to be paved, and the World Bank loaned the government much of the money to do this. Unfortunately much of the land which used to support lush tropical rainforest became useless for farming after a few years. Many new settlers abandoned their land and headed further on into the jungle to see if they had better luck with the next piece of land they cleared.

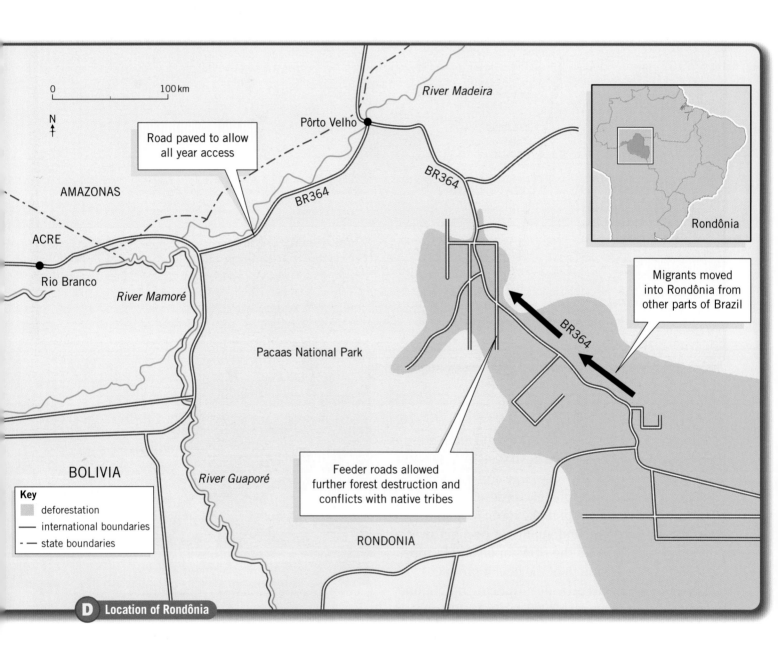

0   100 km

N

Road paved to allow all year access

River Madeira

Pôrto Velho

BR364

AMAZONAS

BR364

ACRE

Rio Branco

River Mamoré

Rondônia

Migrants moved into Rondônia from other parts of Brazil

Pacaas National Park

BR364

BOLIVIA

River Guaporé

Feeder roads allowed further forest destruction and conflicts with native tribes

RONDONIA

Key
- deforestation
- international boundaries
- state boundaries

D Location of Rondônia

E Rainforest destruction in Rondônia – the area shown is 240 km²

Key

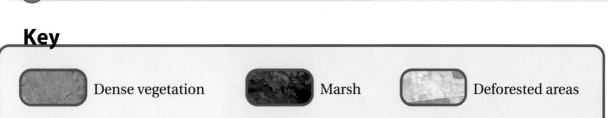

Dense vegetation   Marsh   Deforested areas

Mining in the Amazon jungle

The Amazon has great mineral wealth. One of the largest mining projects is in the Carajás mountains. One of the largest known deposits of iron ore in the world is here. The ore is very pure, containing 66 per cent iron. Since 1980 the Brazilian government has opened up the area. As a result, 100 square kilometres of rainforest have been destroyed. A 900 km railway line to a deep-water port at São Luis has been built to export the iron ore.

The project uses power **generated** by the nearby Tucurui **Hydro power plan**t. Building this meant that another 2000 square kilometres of forest was destroyed. Nearby forest is also under pressure for making charcoal, which is needed to produce the iron. The company that developed the area has now agreed to protect 12 000 square kilometres of land and the native people who live there. In exchange, it wants to mine a further 4120 square kilometres. Many environmentalists ask whether twenty years' supply of iron ore is worth the ecological damage.

Key
- — dam
- factory
- airport
- railway
- Pig iron project
- Charcoal project

F Development at Carajás

G Carajás iron ore mine

How is Brazil changing and what are the impacts of these changes?

Don't re-read every single sentence! Try to skim read and look out for dates quoted in the text.

Activities

1 Draw a timeline to record the important events in Brazil's attempts to develop the country since 1960. You will need to look back over earlier pages of this unit. Set your timeline out like this. Remember to allow lots of space – if things start to get cluttered, use a key.

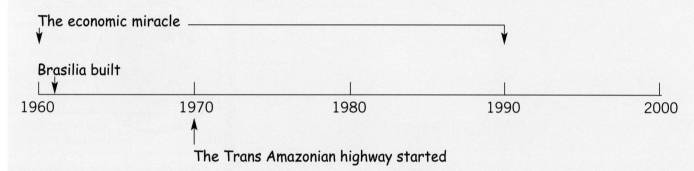

2 Choose a colour for each of the regions you studied earlier in the unit and make a key. For each change that you have marked on your diagram, shade neatly behind the writing to show which part of Brazil was affected.

3 Write a short paragraph to summarise what your timeline diagram shows about the developments that have occurred in Brazil since 1960.

4 Choose three of the changes that you have marked on your diagram. Try to assess how successful each of the developments has been. Set your work out like this.

Development: Sobradinho Reservoir	Region: NE Brazil
Brief description of development:	
Good things about the change:	
Bad things about the change:	
Verdict:	

5 Work out a league table for the developments that you have considered in activity **4**. Put the most successful development first. Write a short summary to describe any pattern that your league table shows.

Review and reflect

Looking at the lives of six Brazilians

My name is Renato and I've had a varied life. My family started off in the south of Brazil, in the State of Parana. We had no land. Then big machinery was brought into the large estate farms and took away the jobs of casual workers. We headed out to Rondônia twenty years ago. I dreamed of owning my own bit of land, but things didn't work out. Here we are in Porto Velho. My son has a small café in the town and I help out when my health allows me. I've never really got used to the climate.

They call me Yano. Things have changed for us over the last twenty years. We have to fight to keep our lands where we used to make a living. We can't catch as many fish as we used to. We can now trade forest products but there is so much pressure to change the forest that our old way of life will soon be a memory.

I'm called Maria. Life has always been difficult here in north-east Brazil. My grandparents farmed in the fertile valley of the São Francisco river. That was before the dam was constructed. I suppose our country needs the electricity. They resettled our family but the land we got wasn't as good. I'm not sure that I can face farming as my parents did.

Map A

0   1000 km

N

Manaus •

Belém •

NORTH

NORTH-EAST

Rondônia •

CENTRE-WEST

Mato Grosso

Brasília •

Belo Horizonte •

SOUTH-EAST

São Paulo •   Rio de Janeiro •

Curitiba •

SOUTH

A

I'm Luiz Boaz and I work as a beef exporter, so I need to be near our headquarters in São Paulo. I live in one of the city centre apartments but am often away on business. Our lifestyle is good – like many other Brazilians, we can afford a live-in maid. Our children go to good schools.

Everyone knows me in my factory; they called me B.A. I suppose I am lucky to have this job. The working conditions are good and everyone is friendly. Pepsi built this factory out in the small provincial town of Jundiai, not too far from São Paulo. Brazil is a great country to live in.

My name is Somália da Silva. I live on the outskirts of Rio de Janeiro in a *favela* called Vigário Geral. It is a tough place in Rio's North Zone. I have six daughters and am pregnant again. We all stay in the room furthest from the street during the night for fear of stray bullets and police raids on the *favela*.

You need to be familiar with all the investigations that you have done on Brazil as you work through these activities. The sections on the regions of Brazil and the developments are especially important. The activities are best done in groups of up to six people.

Activities

1. Read the statements made by the six people on the opposite page. Spend some time within your group deciding who is going to represent each of the six characters. Write down the results of your discussion.

2. For each character that you represent, write a full description of the kind of life they lead.

help!

Start off by using what the character has said on page 66, then think about the following topics which have run through this unit:

- the **location** of where they live within Brazil

- the **natural** environment there, e.g. climate, vegetation and relief

- the **economy** of the area, e.g. the sort of jobs people do

- the **social** geography of the area, e.g. family life, population density, birth and death rate, life expectancy

- the **changes** that are occurring in the area.

3. Copy the table below. Work out a **conflict matrix** for each of the characters:

Somália	Renato	B.A.	Luiz	Maria	Yano
Somália					
	Renato			✓	
		B.A.			
			Luiz		
				Maria	
					Yano

- If you think the two characters would share many of the same interests and agree with each other about how Brazil was being developed, mark with a tick (✓). One has been done for you.
- If you think they would disagree, mark with a cross (✗).
- If you think they would have no strong feeling mark with a wavy line (〰).
- Put two ticks (✓✓) or two crosses (✗✗) if the agreement or disagreement is very great.

4. Give reasons for the decisions you have made in activity **3**. Focus in particular on the character or characters you represent.

5. **Extension**

   Work out a new conflict matrix for how you think things might change over the next ten years. Remember to justify your decisions.

4 France

The changing economic geography of France

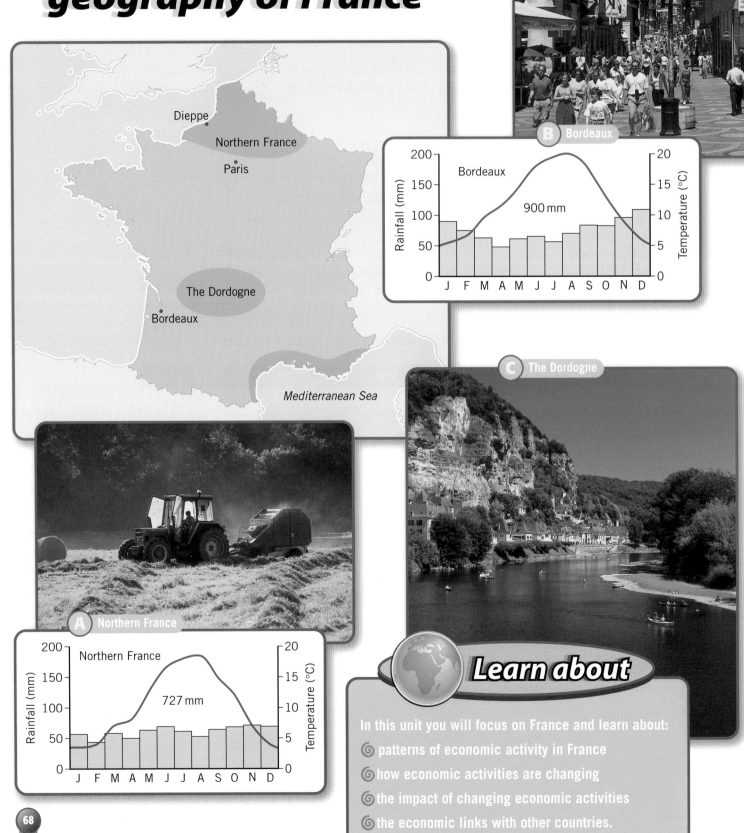

Dieppe

Northern France

Paris

The Dordogne

Bordeaux

Mediterranean Sea

B Bordeaux

Bordeaux
900 mm

Rainfall (mm) / Temperature (°C)
J F M A M J J A S O N D

C The Dordogne

A Northern France

Northern France
727 mm

Rainfall (mm) / Temperature (°C)
J F M A M J J A S O N D

Learn about

In this unit you will focus on France and learn about:

- patterns of economic activity in France
- how economic activities are changing
- the impact of changing economic activities
- the economic links with other countries.

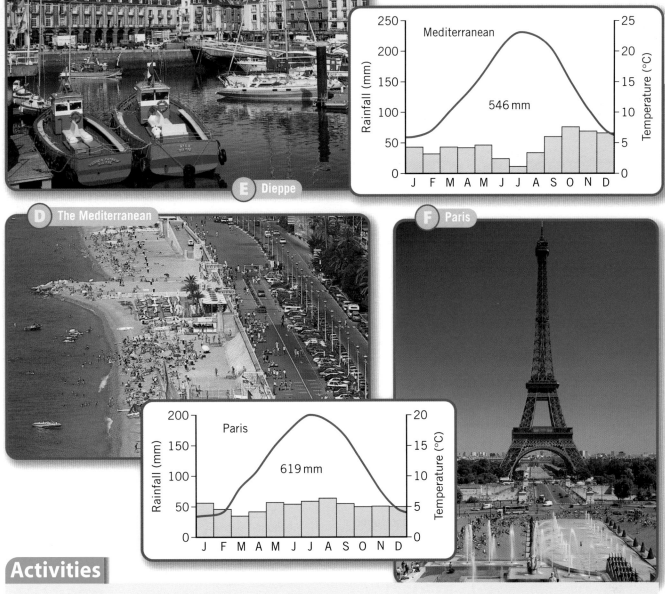

E Dieppe

D The Mediterranean

F Paris

Mediterranean
546 mm

Paris
619 mm

Activities

1 **a** Study the photographs and climate graphs of France.

b Copy and complete the table below to describe the physical and human features of France.

c Research, using an atlas, the weather for **C** and **F**.

	Photo A	Photo B	Photo C
Physical/natural features (e.g. mountains, rivers, trees, hills) Climate (e.g. hot, rainy, sunny)			
Economic activity (e.g. farming, industry, services)			
Settlement (e.g. flats, houses, village, city)			
Population (e.g. lots of people, few people, farmers, tourists)			

2 Use the information in your table. Is there a link between the economic activities of France and the physical environment?

Getting Technical ▼

⑥ **Economic activities** are work or activities that people earn money from.

⑥ **Primary activities** are activities that extract natural resources from the earth or sea.

⑥ **Secondary activities** are activities that process raw materials from primary activities to produce finished goods or semi-finished goods.

⑥ **Tertiary activities** are activities that provide a service.

What is France's economy like? How is it changing?

A Harvesting

B Aeronautics industry

C Café in Paris

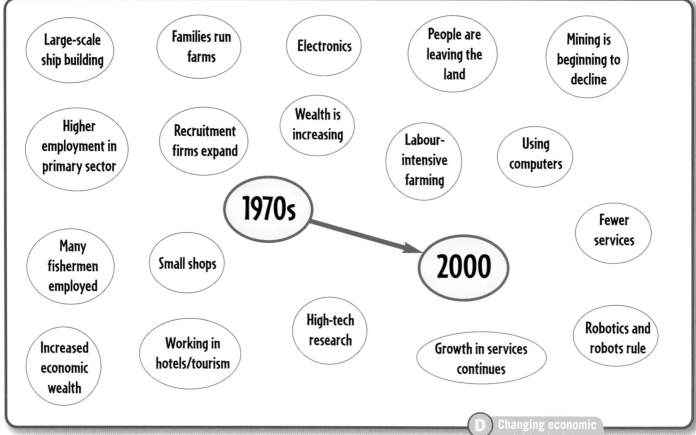

Large-scale ship building

Families run farms

Electronics

People are leaving the land

Mining is beginning to decline

Higher employment in primary sector

Recruitment firms expand

Wealth is increasing

Labour-intensive farming

Using computers

1970s

Many fishermen employed

Small shops

2000

Fewer services

Increased economic wealth

Working in hotels/tourism

High-tech research

Growth in services continues

Robotics and robots rule

D Changing economic activities in France

Activities

1. Match the economic activities in photos **A**, **B** and **C** into primary, secondary and tertiary activities.

2. Classify the phrases in **D** into those that relate to the 1970s and those that relate to 2000.

3. Using your classification, describe how economic activities in the 1970s were different from those in 2000.

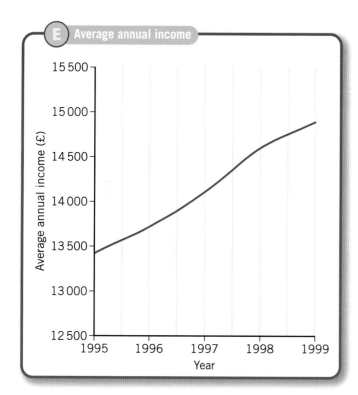

E Average annual income

	1995	1996	1997	1998	1999
Number registered unemployed (thousands)	3000	3100	3100	3000	2800
Unemployment rate (%)	11.6	12.3	12.5	11.8	11.2

G Unemployment statistics

	Oil	Gas	Coal	Electricity	Others
Production	99	35	14	92	11
Consumption	93	34	7	32	9

*Figures in million tonnes of oil equivalent
(ask your teacher if you do not understand this).*

F Energy production and consumption in France, 1999

The number of people out of work in France is high – over 11 per cent of the total working population. The situation is even worse than it appears because:

- many young people stay in education for a long time
- many people are doing their military service.

One reason for unemployment in France is that there are not enough people with the right skills for the jobs available. However, between now and 2010 the number of unemployed people in France will probably fall.

Activities

1. Study graph **E**.
   a What was the average income in 1999?
   b What has been the increase in average income between 1995 and 1999?
   c Between which two years was the biggest increase in annual income?
   d Write a sentence to explain the patterns that the graph shows.

2. Use the data in table **F** to draw a bar chart showing the production and consumption of each type of energy. Copy the outline below and use different colours to show production and consumption, label the axes and add a title at the top of the chart.

3. Read the paragraph above on the right. Use this and the unemployment statistics in table **G** to create a five-minute news flash about unemployment in France.

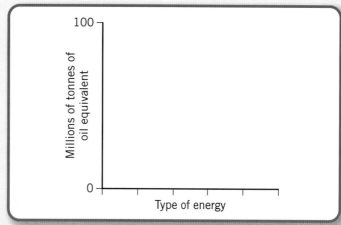

What changes have occurred in the agricultural industry?

Agriculture in France

France has the biggest agricultural industry in Europe. It is the second biggest exporter of agricultural produce in the world behind the USA.

For the past fifty years the number of farmers has been decreasing. In 1970 there were 2.8 million farmers and in 1998 there were just 1.1 million. During the 1990s, 30 000 farmers gave up farming each year.

Despite there being fewer farmers, production has increased. In the 1940s one farmer could produce enough food to feed five people but by 1990 one farmer could produce enough food to feed 30 people.

Production has increased for a number of reasons, including more intensive farming techniques and the use of fertilisers and pesticides.

A An upland farm

France's farming industry has benefited from the support of the European Union. Farmers are given a guaranteed price for their produce as well as grants to help them in many other ways.

However, guaranteed prices meant that farmers were paid money to produce more food, and too much food was produced. This resulted in the 'milk lakes' and 'butter mountains' of the 1980s.

Because of this over-production, support from the European Union is now being reduced. This is resulting in problems in France because the support favours the most efficient farmers who are often the richest and need the least help.

B Intensive farming

Activities

① Read the information about farming in France. Choose five phrases from the text above about changes in agriculture and use them to complete the sentence below:

Agriculture in France is changing ...

② **a** In pairs, consider the following question. You may use the information on this page and the statements on the opposite page, or any knowledge you have about agriculture in France.

Why is the number of farmers in France going down but production is increasing?

b Make a short summary or presentation of your ideas.

Pierre has been adding fertilisers to his crops since 1980.

Jean Claude is guaranteed a set price for all his cows.

Irrigation means that more crops can be grown.

Machinery has made farming a lot quicker.

In 1950 there were 2.3 million farms. In 1990 there were 900 000.

Fabien, my son, lost his job because the farm he worked on bought new machinery.

Guaranteed prices from the European Union have led to over-production.

We use only natural fertilisers on our crops.

There is increasing demand for organically grown food.

Because I use pesticides I lose less of my produce as the bugs that eat the crops are killed.

Seeds and plants are more resistant to diseases now because of genetic engineering.

In 1950 the average farm size was 14 hectares. In 1990 it was 36 hectares.

Advances in technology mean that fewer farmers are needed.

In 1950 there were 5.1 million people working in farming compared to 1.1 million in 1998.

Wine makes up a lot of farming exports for France.

The fishing industry is suffering because of cheap imports.

Fewer farmers are needed now because machines are quicker.

Many people have left their farms to work in the city.

Woodland covers a quarter of France. Some timber is exported but even more is imported.

We are the only family-run farm for 10 km.

Selective breeding programmes mean that only the best animals are produced on my farm.

What changes have occurred in the manufacturing industry?

Case Study

A Grenoble is located in the Rhône-Alpes region

Rhône-Alpes

Grenoble

Getting Technical ▼

A **technopole** is an area with new high-tech industries.

Activities

1. Study the broken sentences in boxes **B** and **C**. To find out *how* and *why* manufacturing industry in the Rhône-Alpes region of France has changed, match the starts of the sentences in box **B** with the endings in box **C**.

2. Imagine you have been sent to interview M. Charvet, the owner of a micro-electronics manufacturing company in Grenoble. You have completed the interview (see box **D**) but have forgotten to write down the questions you asked. Write the questions to match the answers from the interview. The first one has been completed for you.

3. **Extension**

Imagine you are a reporter for a British newspaper and your editor has sent you to France to report on industry in the Rhône-Alpes region.

a Use a desktop publishing or word-processing package to complete this activity.

b The headline is 'Out with the old, in with the new!'

c Lay out your work to look like a real newspaper article. Make up a suitable name for your newspaper and include the headline and your name on the page.

d Use the following paragraph plan when writing your article:

⊚ First paragraph: Say why, what, where, when and who.

⊚ Second paragraph: Give more details about the five points above, and say how.

⊚ Third paragraph: Use a quote from your interview with M. Charvet in Activity 2.

⊚ Fourth, fifth and sixth paragraphs: Include other details from Activity 1.

⊚ Seventh and eighth paragraphs: Write a suitable conclusion.

B

Old heavy industries have been in decline in the region since the oil

Technopoles were set up in Rhône-Alpes

People who did work in the old industries rarely work in the

Technopoles make good profits so

The government has helped the region by giving

Transport routes are good and provide a link between northern and

The Rhône-Alpes region is France's leading producer of

New high-tech industries locate in areas called

C

technopoles, which are like science parks.

money to improve housing and roads.

region in the 1980s.

southern Europe.

they can pay more for rent and taxes.

new industries because they do not have the skills.

manufactured goods.

crisis of 1979.

D

You: *Where and when did you start up your company?*

M. Charvet: I built my micro-electronics factory on the technopole in Grenoble, which is in the Rhône-Alpes region, back in 1986.

You:

M. Charvet: I previously owned a factory which produced oil-based products.

You:

M. Charvet: I was affected by a range of issues – my company didn't recover from the oil crisis of 1979.

You:

M. Charvet: The technopole is a great area to locate – it benefits from being at the centre of networks of motorways, high-speed railways and air routes.

You:

M. Charvet: You can also find the Nuclear Research Centre, the World Health Organization and the Cancer Research Centre here.

You:

M. Charvet: The Lorraine and Nord regions have also suffered from a decline in traditional manufacturing industries.

You:

M. Charvet: The future is bright because the government is actually encouraging technopoles to develop.

What is the pattern of tourism in France?

Activities

A trip to France

- At last! The holidays are here and you are off to travel around France for a fortnight.

- You have been planning your route for months and have investigated six tourist areas in France.

- You will fly from Birmingham to Paris, and catch the ferry home from Calais.

1 You need to choose five areas to visit from the choice of six. You must visit Paris and Boulogne.

2 You need to pack for the trip. Your bag must not weigh more than 6.5 kg (6 500 g) when it is full.

3 For each stage of your journey you need to:

a Decide what you will pack and why.
Use table **A** to help you.

b Decide what you want to see and do at each location and why.

c Calculate the distances between your destinations using table **B**.

d Decide how long you will stay at each location and why.

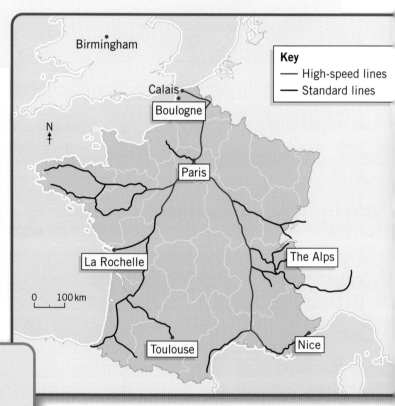

Boulogne

Average July temperature: 22 °C

- White cliffs similar to those at Dover run along the coast between Boulogne and Calais.

- Boulogne's historic buildings include the Palais de Justice, the library and the town hall.

- The wide range of restaurants and shops are well worth a visit.

- Will you visit local hypermarkets before you catch the ferry?

La Rochelle

Average July temperature: 25 °C

- La Rochelle is well known for its historic port.

- The marina is the busiest yachting centre on the French Atlantic.

- Countless cafés and restaurants cluster around the waterfront.

- The cobbled streets of the old town are lined with boutiques.

- The fifteenth-century prison is worth a visit. It has amazing views from the tower.

- You could visit the modern aquarium.

Toulouse

Average July temperature: 25 °C

- The birthplace of Concorde.

- An important industrial and university city.

- You may want to visit Pont Neuf on the River Garonne.

- Tourists are drawn to the two thirteenth-century cathedrals.

- The old town has a lively atmosphere and inexpensive cafés.

- A flea market is held every Sunday.

Paris

Average July temperature: 24 °C

- The spectacular city of Paris has something to offer everyone: from chic shopping to spectacular shows, Paris has it all.
- Paris is the capital of France and the home of fashion.
- The city's highlights include a stroll along the Champs-Élysées from the Arc de Triomphe towards the Louvre, where you could see the *Mona Lisa*.
- You might want to visit the Eiffel Tower or the modern art gallery called Musée d'Orsay.
- You could eat in a gourmet restaurant or enjoy a dinner cruise on the River Seine.

The Alps

Average July temperature: 28 °C

- Stunning scenery combined with fine hospitality.
- From foothills to dramatic peaks, the Alps are a magnet for visitors in summer and winter.
- Skiers need no introduction to this winter playground.
- You might want to try mountain biking or horse riding in the hills.

Nice

Average July temperature: 28 °C

- The two-kilometre golden beach of Nice has to be seen.
- The promenade is lined with palms and has wonderful views.
- The old town has a blend of balconied buildings, and is home to artists, galleries, boutiques and, of course, restaurants.
- You could visit the market.
- You could relax in a pavement café and spend your time people-watching!

Item	Weight (g)	Item	Weight (g)
Water bottle	50	Raincoat	300
Money belt	50	Washing kit	300
Sunglasses	50	Sleeping bag	350
Socks	50	Long skirt	350
Swimsuit/trunks	100	Towel	400
Pack of cards	150	Tracksuit bottoms	400
Deodorant	150	Suntan lotion	400
Hair gel/spray	200	Shampoo	400
Aftershave/perfume	200	Dress	450
Underwear	200	Smart trousers	450
Umbrella	200	Camera and film	500
Shirt/blouse	200	Hairdryer	500
Mountain kit	200	Sleeping mat	500
Sarong	200	Fleece	600
Sandals	200	Jeans	600
Shorts	250	Smart shoes	700
T-shirt	250	Jumper	700
Thermals	250	Trainers	800
Make-up bag	250	Travel guide	1000
Book	300	Walking boots	1000

A Travel kit weight guide

	Boulogne	La Rochelle	Toulouse	Paris	Alps	Nice
Boulogne		350	700	250	550	800
La Rochelle	350		325	350	550	625
Toulouse	700	325		475	400	375
Paris	250	350	475		350	550
Alps	550	550	400	350		300
Nice	800	625	375	550	300	

B Chart to show distances between possible destinations (km)

Activity

4 **Extension**

After your trip you could evaluate your holiday to make next year's journey even better. Use the following sentence starters to help you.

I enjoyed …

As well …

I have learnt that …

Skills I have used include …

For example …

I had a problem with …

Next year I would …

Case Study

Tourism in Rhône-Alpes

It is estimated that 60 million tourists visit France every year, and some of these will visit the Rhône-Alpes region. The Rhône-Alpes region is partly made up of the Alps, but these are just one of the region's tourist attractions. The region attracts tourists in both summer and winter for a number of reasons.

In the east of the region are the Alps and tourists come to ski and snowboard in the winter and walk in the summer.

Tourists come all year round to visit the River Rhône, where they can enjoy lots of watersports and river walks. The area is also famous for its vineyards.

In the south of the region is the Ardèche Gorge, home to many prehistoric caves. The famous Combe d'Arc cave has drawings that are 20 000 years old.

People also come to the region to visit the major cities. In the cities of Grenoble and Lyons tourists soak up the culture by visiting the museums and art galleries as well as eating in the many restaurants and cafés.

A The River Rhône

Activities

1 Read the information about tourism in the Rhône-Alpes region.

   a In one colour, identify five things to do and see in Rhône-Alpes.

   b In another colour, identify five facts about tourism in Rhône-Alpes.

2 In groups of three, take the role of one of the following characters each and present/discuss his or her views about tourism in Rhône-Alpes:

   ⑥ tourist (skier)

   ⑥ environmentalist

   ⑥ business person (for example, hotel or shop owner)

   ⑥ local resident

   ⑥ local councillor.

The three characters should have a conversation about tourism in Rhône-Alpes. Your conversation should be based around the following points:

⑥ whether your character thinks tourism is a good idea

⑥ what your character thinks about the effects that tourism has on the environment

⑥ your character's opinion about the money tourism brings in to the area.

What energy resources does France have?

France as a nation uses many different types of energy. This energy comes from a range of sources.

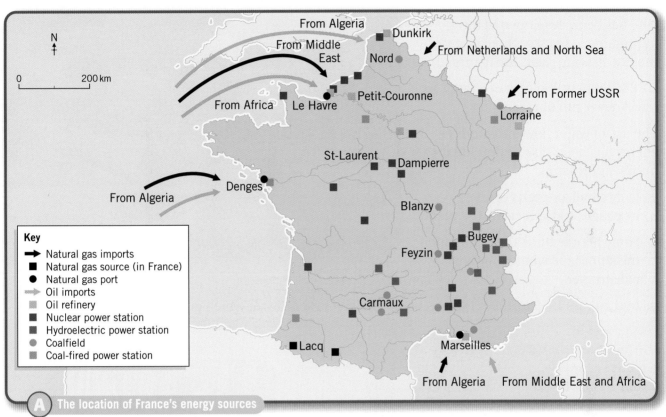

Key
- → Natural gas imports
- ■ Natural gas source (in France)
- ● Natural gas port
- → Oil imports
- ■ Oil refinery
- ■ Nuclear power station
- ■ Hydroelectric power station
- ● Coalfield
- ■ Coal-fired power station

From Algeria
From Middle East
Dunkirk
From Netherlands and North Sea
Nord
From Africa   Le Havre   Petit-Couronne
From Former USSR
Lorraine
St-Laurent   Dampierre
From Algeria   Denges
Blanzy
Bugey
Feyzin
Carmaux
Lacq   Marseilles
From Algeria   From Middle East and Africa

A The location of France's energy sources

Coal

- Coal was a very important source of energy in France until recently.

- In 1958, 60 million tonnes were produced – 60 per cent of the total energy used in France.

- In 1958, 300 000 miners were employed.

- By 1989, only 13 million tonnes were produced each year and only 28 000 miners were employed.

- The last mine on one of the main coalfields, Nord-Pas-de-Calais, closed in 1991. It was expensive to mine coal there and the type of coal was bad for the miners' health. The environment in this area has been badly affected by spoil tips, derelict mine buildings, and water and air pollution.

B Coal mining in France

Hydroelectric power (HEP)

- HEP has been welcomed by many people in France as it is a non-polluting source of energy.

- HEP has been developed in the mountains of France where many of the fast-flowing rivers are dammed.

- HEP is a renewable type of energy, so it will never run out.

- The use of water power to produce energy has been slow to develop for a number of reasons:

  - Only small amounts of energy can be produced from each HEP plant.

  - Some people think the plants spoil the landscape where they are constructed.

  - In the years 1989 to 1990 HEP was badly affected by a drought which greatly reduced output.

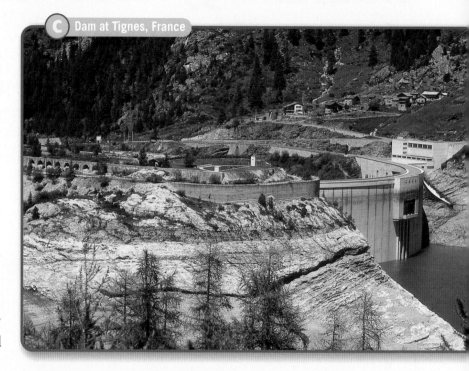
C Dam at Tignes, France

Gas and oil

- Gas and oil are important sources of energy and both are used to generate electricity.

- Gas and oil are both fossil fuels and have two main disadvantages:

  - They are non-renewable (they will run out over time).

  - They cause air pollution.

- Most of the gas and oil used in France is imported from Russia and the Netherlands.

- Since the oil crises in the 1970s, France has cut back on its use of oil.

D Gas pipeline, Manosque

E Drilling for oil

Nuclear power

- Nuclear power is the main source of France's energy resources.

- In 1974 the French government began to invest in nuclear power stations.

- It takes seven years to build a nuclear reactor, so it was not until the early 1980s that nuclear power could be used.

- There are problems regarding nuclear waste – where should it be stored?

- Nuclear power stations tend to be located near a water source, which is used for cooling.

- Nuclear power has its advantages – it is very efficient and relatively cheap to make.

- The cost of building nuclear power generators is huge. These costs have led to huge debts for Electricité de France. The state electricity company had a debt of £25.4 billion by 1990.

F Nuclear power station at St Alban–St Maurice, on the River Rhône

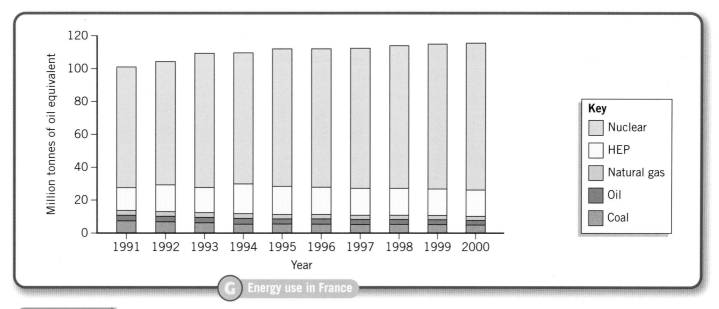

G Energy use in France

Activities

1. Using the information on each type of energy, create a timeline from 1958 to 2001 to show the changes in energy use in France.

2. Copy and complete the table below to show the advantages and disadvantages of each type of energy.

Energy source	Advantages	Disadvantages

3. Using graph **G**, draw your own graph to estimate France's energy use between 2000 and 2010. Explain the energy use you have predicted.

France's energy mix – the nuclear power debate

A Nuclear power station in the Loire valley

B

Nuclear power is now the main source of ...

A tidal power station has also been built ...

In 1974 the French government began to ...

There are lots of problems connected with the storage of nuclear waste because ...

Nuclear power stations tend to be located near a water ...

Nuclear power uses uranium – the amount needed is small ...

HEP has been developed in the mountains ...

Recently some people have started to worry about ...

invest in nuclear power stations.

at Rance in Normandy.

energy in France today.

whether nuclear power is safe.

no one wants it in their neighbourhood.

and the cost is relatively low.

where many of the fast-flowing rivers are dammed.

source, which is used for cooling.

C

Activities

1 Study the broken sentences in boxes **B** and **C**.

   a Match the starts of the sentences in box **B** with the endings in box **C**.

   b There are two sentences which have nothing to do with nuclear power. Find these 'odd ones out' and write them down in a separate list from the sentences about nuclear power.

2 Read the newspaper article in box **D**. People have a wide range of views about any debate. Some views are based on fact, others on opinion, and some may be a mixture of both.

   a Write down the facts in one colour and the opinions in another colour.

   b Share your facts and opinions with others in your group. How did you decide what was a fact and what was an opinion?

LIFE IN THE SHADOW OF A NUCLEAR POWER STATION

Back in 1952 Madame Goma bought a house in the town of Dampierre. Today, she has a very different neighbour …

I met Madame Goma at her home and we discussed how the energy situation in France had changed over time and how it had affected her life.

During the 1970s the French economy was negatively affected by two oil crises. In 1974 the French government decided to build 34 nuclear reactors, followed in 1976 by a further 20. Today nuclear energy represents 75 per cent of the country's electricity production.

I asked Madame Goma what it was like living next to a nuclear power station.

'I feel safe living next to the station because of the very high standard of nuclear safety at the site, and other similar sites in France. I often see officials from the Ministry of Health around the site checking for radioactive releases from the site.'

Madame Goma felt that the site had also had a negative impact upon her life. 'The value of my house has suffered because it is so close to the site, and the continual noise of vehicles in and out of the station is a nuisance.'

Nuclear power has been very successful in France and it seems that it is likely to be so in the future. However, this source of energy is always a controversial issue, having as many disadvantages as advantages.

I doubt that everyone shares the opinions of Madame Goma. I'm sure the nuclear debate will continue for many years to come.

D

Activity

3 **Extension**

Using all of the information from these pages, write a newspaper article examining how people feel about the use of nuclear power in France. Write your article from the viewpoint of one of the following people:

- environmental campaigner
- government official
- official from the nuclear power plant
- a worker from one of the plants.

help!

Use four sections to structure your article:

- ✪ *Introduction* – write a paragraph to explain what the newspaper report is about.
- ✪ *Background* – describe where, when and why nuclear power stations have been built.
- ✪ *Current situation* – describe in detail the current situation.
- ✪ *Closing statement* – what are the consequences and how are you affected by what has happened?

Remember that all these people are affected by nuclear power in different ways and they may have differing opinions on this source of energy.

International trade

International trade is the buying and selling of goods between countries. Goods brought into a country are called imports and goods sold to other countries are called exports. The difference between the value of imports and the value of exports is called the balance of trade. This may vary from year to year.

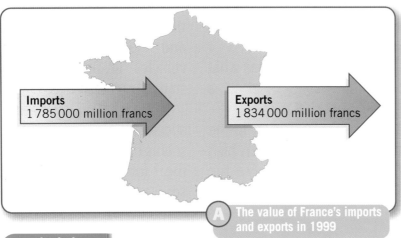

Imports
1 785 000 million francs

Exports
1 834 000 million francs

A The value of France's imports and exports in 1999

Activities

1. Create a word bank of the key words and terms in the text above – *international trade, imports, exports* and *balance of trade*.

2. Work out France's balance of trade in 1999 by subtracting the value of imports from the value of exports.

3. In 1999 France had a positive balance of trade. Read the first paragraph again, then explain why the balance of trade shows France has a healthy economy.

France's exports

The goods exported from France in 1999 are shown in graph **B**.

		%
Raw materials, metals, chemicals		32
Machines and equipment for industry		25
Consumer goods		14
Cars and trucks		14
Food industry products		9
Farm, forestry and fishing products		4
Energy products		2

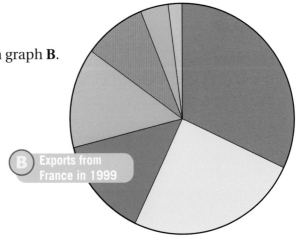

B Exports from France in 1999

France is famous for its exports of food products, clothes and cars. For example, nearly a quarter of cars sold in Europe are French. France's exports of high-tech goods are growing – an example is the aircraft industry, based at Toulouse.

France's imports

		%
Raw materials, metals, chemicals		33
Machines and equipment for industry		23
Consumer goods		16
Cars and trucks		11
Energy products		7
Food industry products		7
Farm, forestry and fishing products		3

The goods France imported in 1999 are shown in graph **C**. Some imports like food products are used directly by the people, sometimes called **consumers**. Other imports such as chemicals are used by French industries to make other goods.

C Imports to France in 1999

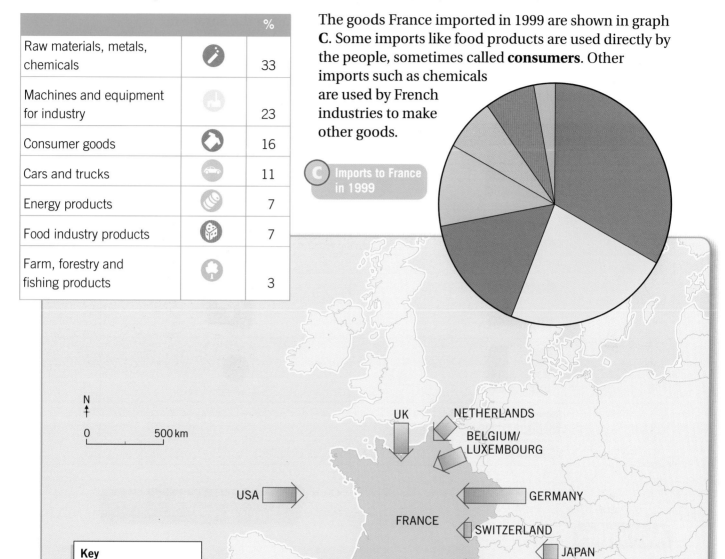

D France's main trading partners for imports in 1999

Key

1 mm = 1 %

N

0   500 km

UK   NETHERLANDS   BELGIUM/LUXEMBOURG   GERMANY   SWITZERLAND   JAPAN   ITALY   FRANCE   USA   SPAIN

Activities

4 **a** Copy the table below, then use graph **C** to work out which imports are for consumers, which are used by industry, or both.

b Work out the total percentage for each category. **123**

	Goods	%
Imports for consumers		
Imports for industry		
Imports for consumers and industry		

5 Compare the figures for exports and imports in graphs **B** and **C**. Make three lists of goods:

- Imports to France greater than exports
- Exports from France greater than imports
- Imports to France similar to exports.

6 Study map **D**. Write a short paragraph about the countries where France imports most goods from. You should mention:

- The top three importing countries
- The overall pattern of imports
- Any other interesting points you notice.

France and the European Union

France has economic links with a range of countries. Being part of the European Union means that taxes are not put on goods imported from other EU countries, so these countries form France's major trading partners. France also has trade links with countries that used to be French colonies. Taxes on goods from these countries are usually lower, making them cheaper than goods from other countries.

		% of value			% of value
Germany		16	Belgium/ Luxembourg		8
UK		10	Netherlands		8
Spain		9	Switzerland		4
Italy		9	Japan		2
USA		8			

E France's main trading partners for exports in 1999

Activities

7 Draw a map with proportional arrows showing France's main export partners, using the data in table **E**.
  - Set your work out like map **D** on page 85.
  - Try using this scale for your arrows: 1 mm = 1 per cent of value.

8 Imagine you work for the French Department of Trade and Industry. It is your job to write a report about trade in France. The title of your report is 'France has a good balance of trade'.

help!

Use the following structure for your report:

- You will need an introduction to explain what your report is about. Use the following starters and write clear, short sentences:
  - This is a report about …
  - In this report I will cover …
  - These are the issues to be discussed …
  - As a country we have …

- Write a few paragraphs to state who France trades with and describe the patterns of France's international trade. Think about:
  - Who are France's main trading partners?
  - What are the main imports/exports?
  - What is France's balance of trade like?

- Include values and statistics in your report.

- In your conclusion explain why France has a good balance of trade.

Review and reflect

FRANCE
Europe
school

ENERGY
reserves
power

AGRICULTURE
farming
land

PARIS
London
capital city

TECHNOPOLE
Grenoble
science park

THE ALPS
mountains
East

MANUFACTURING
industry
secondary

TERTIARY
industry
high-tech

NUCLEAR
energy
power

ECONOMY
money
country

Activities

1 In groups of four, read the cards above.

a Choose one of the cards and describe the word in capitals to the other members of your group *without using any of the other words on the card.*

b Choose another card and draw a picture to represent the word in capitals.

c Design some other cards to try out in your group.

2 Add key words and terms you have used to your word bank. You could start with the words on the cards above.

5 Comparing countries

What do we do when we compare countries?

Comparing two or more countries means studying the countries side by side to see how far they are similar and how far they are different. By comparing two countries we will end up with a much better understanding of both countries.

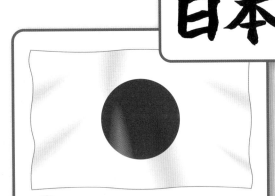

B Japan

日本

中国

A China, the Middle Kingdom

C

D

Learn about

What is it really like to live in another country? Every country is different, but why are countries different? Why do parts of some countries seem very familiar? Finding out about and comparing places is an important geographical skill. In this unit you will learn:

- about two countries in different states of economic development – China and Japan
- how and why China and Japan are geographically similar
- how and why China and Japan are geographically different
- why places such as China and Japan change
- how countries such as China and Japan are linked together
- how to locate places and environments.

1 Before you begin finding out about another country, you need to think about what you already know or do not know about that country. You have learned about **perceptions** before – think carefully about country **stereotyping**.

a Make two lists, one for China and one for Japan. Write down in each list anything you already know about each country (e.g. main cities, industrial company names, sports personalities, people, events).

b Share your lists with a partner. How do they compare?

c Write down ten questions that you would like to ask to find out more about China and Japan.

d Can you think of any reasons why the Chinese name for China is 'the Middle Kingdom'?

2 Look at photographs **C–H**.

a For the photographs that show people, decide what the people are doing (e.g. working, travelling, shopping, on holiday).

b For each photograph, study the landscape. What is it like? Classify them into types (e.g. flat, mountainous, countryside, built up, urban).

c Which photographs do you think were taken in China and which were taken in Japan? Write down where you think each one was taken and give a reason for your choice. (The actual locations of the photographs are given on page 110 – but don't cheat!)

d Write a suitable caption for each photograph.

Where are China and Japan?

The first step of any geographical enquiry is to ask questions. Often the first question you need to ask is 'where are the places located?' You need maps, atlases and globes at a variety of different scales to answer this question fully.

Simply stating that China and Japan are both in the continent of Asia begins to locate these countries, but we can define them more accurately using lines of latitude and longitude.

Using map **A** we can see that China is between 20°N and 55°N (lines of latitude) and between 75°E and 135°E (lines of longitude).

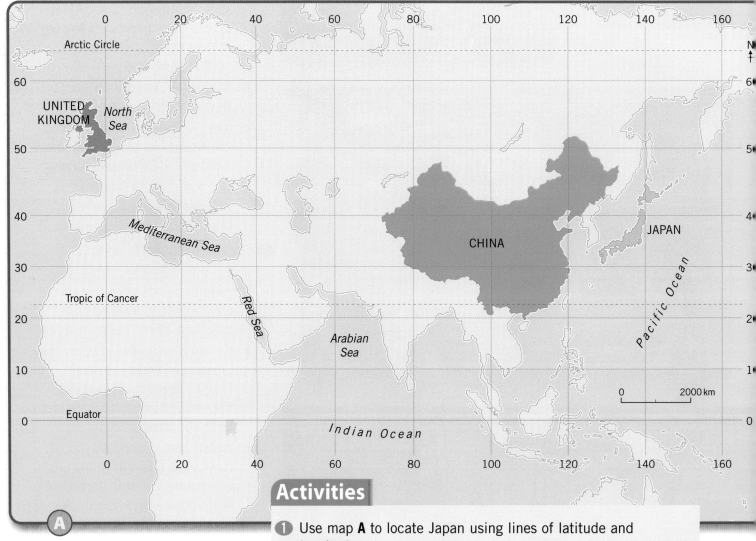

A

Country	Land area (km²)
UK	244 880
China	9 596 960
Japan	377 800

B How much land?

Activities

1. Use map **A** to locate Japan using lines of latitude and longitude.

2. Estimate the central point of China and work out the latitude and longitude of this point. Do the same for Japan.

3. Look up China and Japan in the index of an atlas. What latitude and longitude reference is given for each country? Why do you think they give these references?

4. Work out the location of the UK using latitude and longitude.

Country	Average population density (people per km²)	Total population (millions of people)
UK	237	59
China	126	1259
Japan	332	126

C How many people?

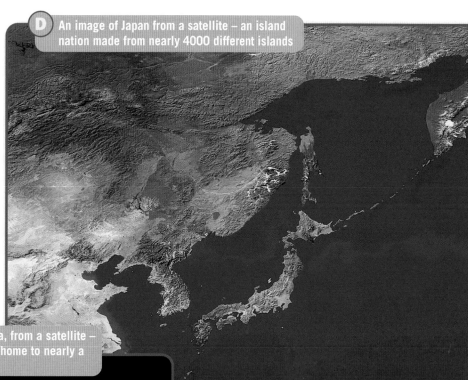

D An image of Japan from a satellite – an island nation made from nearly 4000 different islands

E An image of the world, including China, from a satellite – China is a country large enough to be home to nearly a quarter of the world's population

help!

○ Remember that we are comparing these countries. How much bigger is China than Japan? How much larger is the population of China than that of Japan? Include this information in your summary paragraph.

Activities

5 Study satellite images **D** and **E**. With the help of your atlas, make a list of the oceans and seas that surround the islands of Japan.

6 Make a list of the countries that have a border with China.

7 Write a short paragraph to summarise your answer to the question '*Where are China and Japan?*'

China – where do people live and work?

1 056 666	a month
243 846	a week
34 835	a day
1 451	an hour
24	a minute

A The increase in the Chinese population, 1996

The second step in a geographical enquiry is to decide what data is needed to answer the questions set out in Step one.

In 1999 the Chinese government estimated the population of China to be 1259 million, nearly one quarter of the world's population. The number of people affects every aspect of daily life, from family size, providing homes and jobs, to using resources. The population continues to increase (diagram **A**), even though the rate of increase has slowed down.

China's population is not evenly distributed throughout the country. In 2001 70 per cent of the people live in rural areas, while 30 per cent live in urban areas. However, this is changing and by 2025 the urban population is expected to be bigger than the rural population.

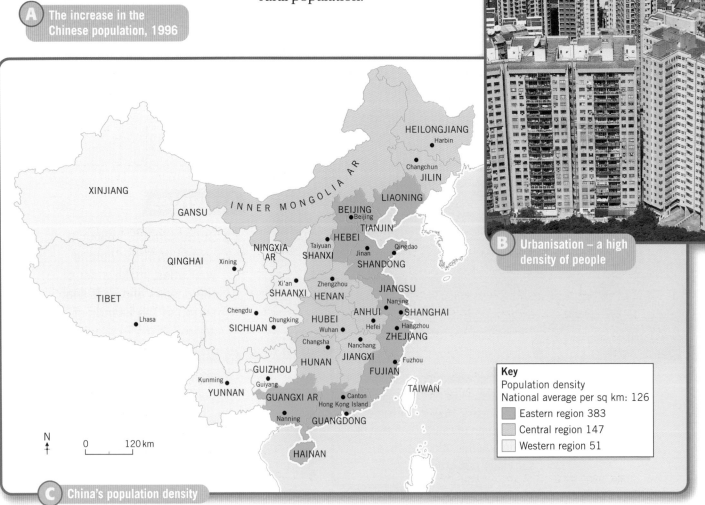

B Urbanisation – a high density of people

Key
Population density
National average per sq km: 126
- Eastern region 383
- Central region 147
- Western region 51

C China's population density

D Rural areas – a low density of people

When the People's Republic of China was established in 1949, there was virtually no agricultural or industrial development. People's average life expectancy was just 32 years. Now China has one of the fastest-growing global economies: in 1990 it was the fifteenth largest trading nation in the world; by 1994 it was eleventh and by 1997, including Hong Kong, it was the fourth largest trading nation in the world. There are still differences between rural and urban living standards, but the average life expectancy is now 70 years.

F A wide range of products are made in China

E The changing nature of work, 1952–1996

Key
- Agriculture
- Manufacturing
- Services

Year	Agriculture	Manufacturing	Services
1952	83.5%	7.4%	9.1%
1965	81.5%	8.3%	10.2%
1978	70.5%	17.4%	12.1%
1986	60.9%	21.9%	17.2%
1991	59.8%	21.4%	18.8%
1996	50.5%	23.5%	26%

Activities

1. Study map **C**.

   a Some parts of China have very few people. Write down the names of these areas.

   b Some parts of China have very many people. List the names of these areas.

   c Use an atlas to find where the main towns and cities are located. By 2025 it is expected that more people will live in cities than in rural areas. What do you think this will mean for the distribution of population?

2. Study graph **E**.

   a Describe what has happened to the number of people who work in agriculture.

   b Describe what has happened to the number of people who work in manufacturing and services.

   c Where in China do you think it would be easier for people to find jobs – the east or the west? Explain why you think so.

   d What difference will increased urbanisation make to the sorts of jobs that are available?

3. Write a short paragraph to summarise what you have found out about:

   a Changes in where people live.

   b Changes in jobs.

Case Study
What do we learn about China from the media?

A China Town in Liverpool

What is the media?

The **media** is any method of communication which reaches large numbers of people. Sometimes stories in the media are not the whole story. The story or image of a place or country often just reflects what the person writing the newspaper article, or making the TV programme, thinks about the country. How does China come across in the media? If you only knew about China from information in the media, what sort of place would you think it is?

Technical achievements in ceramics
Chinese potters were making china that was fired to high temperatures of over 1200 °C nearly 3500 years ago – the Shang dynasty. It took more than 3000 years before countries in the western world developed the technical expertise to make similar china. High-fired, high-quality pottery is still called china. It is usually made from a type of very pure white clay called porcelain.

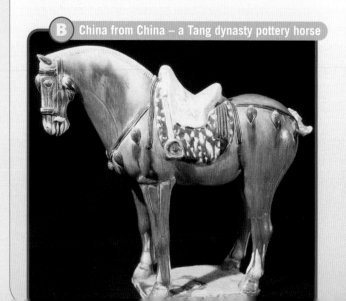

B China from China – a Tang dynasty pottery horse

US to warn Beijing over stalled trade talks

The Times, 12 October 2000

In the jaws of the Dragon

The Guardian, 3 April 2001

China to build world's tallest dam

The Guardian, 15 May 2001

UK exporters fear Chinese uncertainty

The Times, 5 April 2001

China's dustbowl nightmare

The Guardian, 13 June 2001

China puts US in check

The Guardian, 5 April 2001

China puts gloss on labour camps to pacify West

The Daily Telegraph, 20 May 2001

China anger at British attacks on human rights

The Daily Telegraph, 1 December 2000

 C What the papers say

---

1 Renminbi	= 100 Yuan
12 Renminbi	= £1

 **D** Chinese currency

Activities

1. Study photograph **A**. Make a list of the things that make this place distinctive as China Town. Who are these things for – the local people or tourists?

2. Read the fact file. Does China's long history of technical expertise match the image of China in the newspaper headlines (**C**)?

3. Study the newspaper headlines in **C**. Annotate each headline to show how China is portrayed. An example is given below.

In the jaws of the Dragon

Why Dragon? The Chinese five-toed dragon is a symbol of happiness and good fortune. The Dragon stands for a wild, untamed, fierce creature in western cultures. The headline reflects an image of China as powerful (the jaws), mysterious and uncontrollable. In the West the headline is a threatening one. In China it would be difficult to understand. What does this say about the West's image of China? Why is it described in this way? Is China really like that?

4. The newspaper headlines in **C** will soon become out of date. Carry out your own newspaper search for headlines about China over a period of two or three weeks. Make a display of the headlines and annotate each one to explain how China is portrayed in each one. Your school library may have resources to help you.

5. Work in a small group to expand your media search. Monitor radio and TV news and compare the results.

6. Carry out an Internet search to find news articles on China. You could try the websites for:

   ⑥ *BBC News*

   ⑥ *CNN News*

   ⑥ *Electronic Telegraph*

   ⑥ *Guardian Unlimited*

   ⑥ *Yahoo News*

   at www.heinemann.co.uk/hotlinks

China – the physical environment

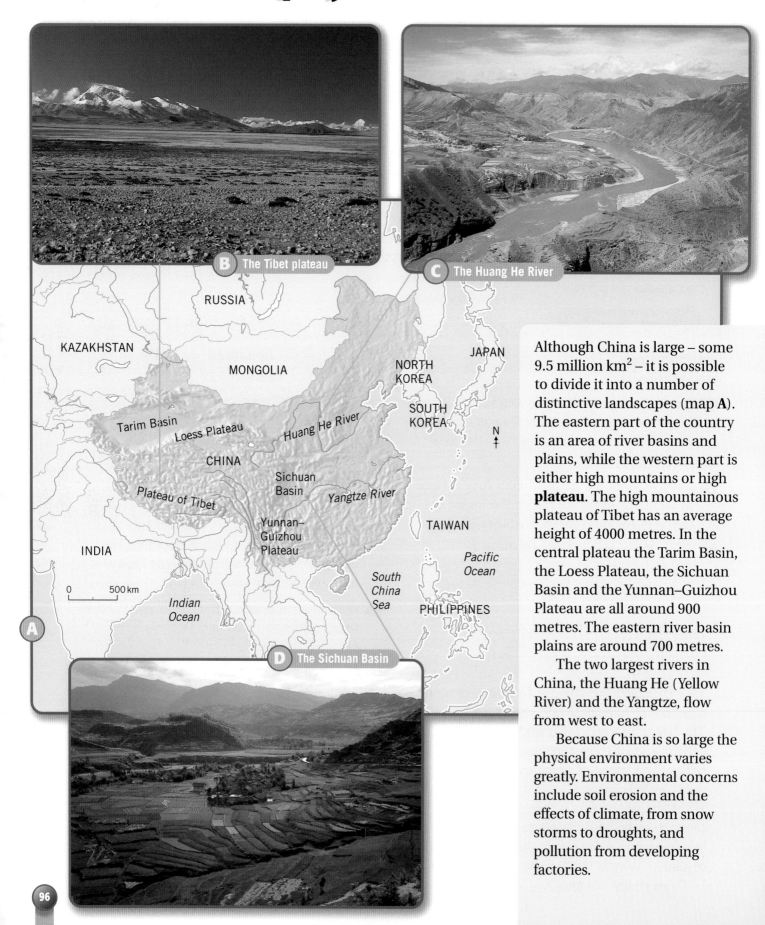

B The Tibet plateau

C The Huang He River

D The Sichuan Basin

Although China is large – some 9.5 million km² – it is possible to divide it into a number of distinctive landscapes (map **A**). The eastern part of the country is an area of river basins and plains, while the western part is either high mountains or high **plateau**. The high mountainous plateau of Tibet has an average height of 4000 metres. In the central plateau the Tarim Basin, the Loess Plateau, the Sichuan Basin and the Yunnan–Guizhou Plateau are all around 900 metres. The eastern river basin plains are around 700 metres.

The two largest rivers in China, the Huang He (Yellow River) and the Yangtze, flow from west to east.

Because China is so large the physical environment varies greatly. Environmental concerns include soil erosion and the effects of climate, from snow storms to droughts, and pollution from developing factories.

Flooding

China is such a large country that localised flooding can take place in all parts of the country, but each year flooding occurs on the Yangtze and Huang He rivers. In 1998 the worst flooding for 44 years occurred in Hubei province. Torrential rains in July and August created a lake seven metres deep and covering nearly 325 km². More than 3000 people were killed, 2.9 million houses were destroyed and more than 9 million hectares of crops were ruined. Flood waters washed away a 3000-metre section of a newly constructed flood protection dike. Officials said that floods, landslides and mudflows affected some 240 million people – one fifth of China's population.

Fire

Forest fires during the hot dry season can cause widespread damage. A total of 3021 people were killed and 4404 others injured in fires in China in 2000. Financial losses were more than 1.5 billion Yuan. The official Xinhua news agency said that tree felling as well as soil erosion following forest fires may have contributed to the flooding. Without the forest cover, rain flows quickly into the rivers, carrying large amounts of soil which silt up the river channels and cause flooding.

F Earthquake damage at Zhangjiapo village, China

Earthquakes

China sits between two of the largest tectonic plate boundaries – the Pacific plate boundary lies to the east and the circum–Indian plate boundary lies to the south west. Since 1900 there have been more than 800 earthquakes of a magnitude of 6.0 or greater on the Richter scale.

China has had some success with predicting earthquakes. Even so, since 1900 nearly half a million people have died in earthquakes – 53 per cent of all the world's earthquake casualties.

On 10 January 1998 an earthquake of 6.2 on the Richter scale caused damage to more than nineteen cities and affected nearly 170 000 people in Zhangbei, Shangyi, Wanquan and Kangding. Forty-nine people were killed and 11 439 people were injured. The economic loss was put at 794 million Yuan.

Activity

1 Copy and complete the hazard grid below. The first row has been done for you – add flooding, fire and earthquakes. You may want to leave some boxes blank.

Hazard	Natural causes	Human causes	Effects	Location or details of damage
Soil erosion	Heavy rain and steep slopes	Deforestation	Soil washed away	Widespread in China

Are there regional differences within China?

It is clear that China has some parts of the country that are different from other parts of the country. But can you clearly identify these regions?

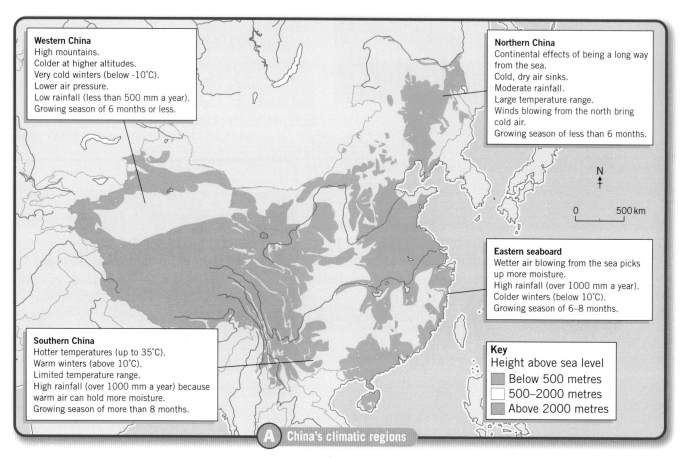

Western China
High mountains.
Colder at higher altitudes.
Very cold winters (below -10°C).
Lower air pressure.
Low rainfall (less than 500 mm a year).
Growing season of 6 months or less.

Northern China
Continental effects of being a long way from the sea.
Cold, dry air sinks.
Moderate rainfall.
Large temperature range.
Winds blowing from the north bring cold air.
Growing season of less than 6 months.

N

0   500 km

Eastern seaboard
Wetter air blowing from the sea picks up more moisture.
High rainfall (over 1000 mm a year).
Colder winters (below 10°C).
Growing season of 6–8 months.

Southern China
Hotter temperatures (up to 35°C).
Warm winters (above 10°C).
Limited temperature range.
High rainfall (over 1000 mm a year) because warm air can hold more moisture.
Growing season of more than 8 months.

Key
Height above sea level
Below 500 metres
500–2000 metres
Above 2000 metres

A China's climatic regions

What do we mean by a region?

Geographers often try to classify different parts of countries into regions. The idea is to identify the features that make each area different. Of course, the real world does not always fit this idea of clear regions easily. For example, some features like climate or relief are easy to measure. Others, such as language differences, or political and economic characteristics, can be more difficult to identify. It is often difficult to know where one region ends and another begins – how do you draw lines in real places?

Activities

1. Map **A** shows detailed information on climate for four regions of China. Copy and complete the table below to summarise the climate in each region. Add figures if you can!

	Rainfall	Temperature	Growing season
Western China			
Southern China			
Eastern seaboard			
Northern China			

2. For each of the regions, work out the height of the land above sea level. How do you think this affects the climate?

N
0   500 km

XINJIANG
GANSU
INNER MONGOLIA AR
HEILONGJIANG
JILIN
LIAONING
BEIJING
TIANJIN
HEBEI
NINGXIA AR
SHANXI
SHANDONG
QINGHAI
SHAANXI   HENAN
JIANGSU
TIBET
ANHUI   SHANGHAI
HUBEI
SICHUAN
ZHEJIANG
HUNAN   JIANGXI
GUIZHOU   FUJIAN
YUNNAN
GUANGXI AR   TAIWAN
GUANGDONG
HAINAN

Key
	1–5
	6–10
	11–15
	16–20
	21–25
	26–30

B The United Nations Human Development Index (HDI) is based upon life expectancy, educational levels and income. This map shows the Chinese provinces ranked according to this index, where 1 is the best and 30 the worst

One country – two systems

In 1997 Hong Kong Island and the surrounding islands were returned to China as a Special Administrative Region (SAR). Some 6.2 million people live in the Hong Kong SAR. In the 1980s and 1990s Hong Kong developed a **democratic** system of government, which was one of the reasons why it has become a major economic centre. China still has a **centralised Communist** system of government. China calls this 'one country – two systems'.

Activities

3 a Study map **B** and work out which provinces have the best HDI.

b Now look back at map **C** on page 92 showing population density. Are the provinces with the best HDI those that have low population densities or high population densities?

4 a On a base map of China, shade the three physical regions (lowlands, plateau and mountains).

b Make a series of three or four overlay maps. The first should show the areas of high population density and the major cities. What could you decide to show on the other overlays – climate, economic development, political provinces, HDI?

c Once you have completed your map and overlays, try to identify any different regions within China.

5 Imagine you have been asked to give a five-minute talk to your local regional twinning organisation. Choose one of the regions you have investigated and write the script for your talk. Make sure you compare this region and your own.

6 **Extension**

a What sort of information do you need to compare regions?

b How does this differ from the information you need to compare countries?

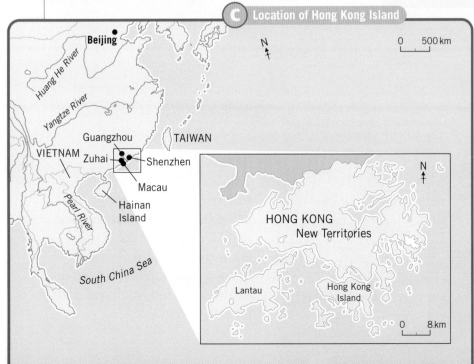

C Location of Hong Kong Island

Beijing
Huang He River
Yangtze River
Guangzhou   TAIWAN
VIETNAM   Zuhai
Shenzhen
Macau
Hainan Island
Pearl River
South China Sea

N
0   500 km

HONG KONG
New Territories
Lantau   Hong Kong Island
0   8 km

D Hong Kong Island

Are there regional differences within Japan?

Just as Britain is divided into counties for local government, Japan is divided into 47 prefectures. These **prefectures** are then grouped into eight regions (map **A**).

Hokkaido

The most northern island. Very few people live here. Jobs are mostly in farming and fishing, although tourism is becoming important.

Tohoku

Honshu Island has five regions. Tohoku is the furthest in the north. It is Japan's main rice-growing region. It has recently been linked to other regions by a new expressway and bullet train. Sendai is becoming a centre for industry and offices.

Chūbu

In the south along the Pacific coast it is mostly urban and industrial. The central mountainous areas are national parks that are easily accessible to many people. To the north, along the coast of the Sea of Japan, many nuclear power stations have been built.

Hokkaido

N

Tohoku

Chūbu

Kanto

Chugoku

Kinki

Kyushu

Shikoku

0   250 km

A Japan's prefectures and regions

Kyushu

The north of the island, which has very good links to Honshu, is an old industrial area. Two-thirds of the population of the island live here. The south is mainly farming, but it is also popular with tourists who come for the sub-tropical climate and volcanic scenery.

Shikoku

This is the smallest of the four main islands. New bridges are being built to connect Shikoku and Honshu, and these will allow the northern coast to become developed. The rest of the island is mountainous and remote.

Kanto

The largest concentration of population live in this region. Tokyo, the capital city, is a centre for manufacturing and service industries. The country's main port is at Yokohama. Kawasaki is one of the main areas for heavy industry. This region is sometimes called the 'heart' of Japan.

Chugoku

This region is remote and underdeveloped. The main city is Hiroshima. Inland it is mountainous.

Kinki

This is Japan's second most important industrial region. It contains three major cities: Kyoto, Osaka and Kobe.

Activities

1. Research photos of Shikoku and Kyushu from the internet or a CD-ROM encyclopedia. Print each photo and annotate them from the information on page 100.

2. Use the photographs and information on these pages to list the physical and human features of the four islands of Hokkaido, Honshu, Shikoku and Kyushu. Copy the table below to help you to organise your ideas. Hokkaido has been started for you.

3. Choose two photographs which you think show the contrasts between the different regions in Japan. Draw a sketch of each photograph and add annotations to show the contrasts in physical and human features.

4. New road and rail links are planned to link Hokkaido with Honshu. How do you think this might change Hokkaido?

Island	Physical features	Human features
Hokkaido	The photograph shows ...	Few people ...
Honshu		
Shikoku		
Kyushu		

Japan – the physical environment

Most of Japan's islands are steep and mountainous so they are of little use for settlement. There are four main islands and about 3900 smaller ones. In fact, less than sixteen per cent of the country is classed as lowland. It is in this small area of lowland that settlement and economic activity must take place. Flat land is a scarce resource in Japan (map **A**).

The steep mountains that make up the 'backbone' of the four main islands are the result of movements between the tectonic plates. When the plates move, the result is often an earthquake or volcanic activity. Sometimes underwater earthquakes cause huge waves called *tsunami*.

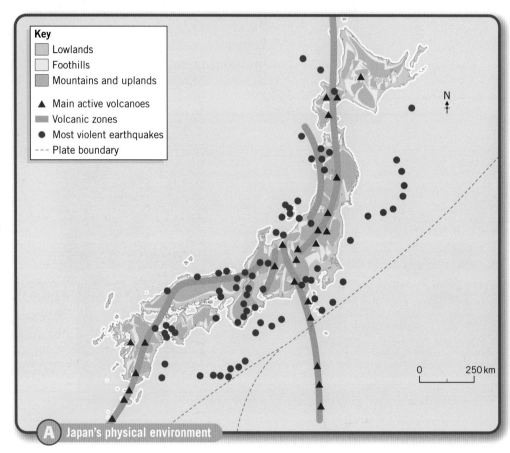

Key
- Lowlands
- Foothills
- Mountains and uplands
- ▲ Main active volcanoes
- Volcanic zones
- ● Most violent earthquakes
- --- Plate boundary

N

0   250 km

A Japan's physical environment

Activities

1 The physical environment of Japan has provided both opportunities and difficulties for the Japanese people. Copy and complete the table below to balance each of the opportunities with the difficulties people face.

2 a Draw up a hazard grid for Japan like the one on page 97. Use the information on page 103 to complete it.

b What differences do you notice between hazards in China and Japan?

Opportunities	Difficulties
Timber resources from the wooded mountains	
Hot springs in the volcanic areas	
Wilderness areas with spectacular scenery to encourage tourists	
A good climate for growing crops	
Fishing in the coastal waters around the islands	

Earthquakes

Kobe (left) is the sixth largest city in Japan. On 17 January 1995 it was shaken by a series of earthquakes. The largest reached 7.2 on the Richter scale. It was Japan's worst earthquake for almost 75 years. Nearly 6000 people were killed, some 26 000 were injured and up to 310 000 were left homeless. Some 75 000 buildings were damaged or destroyed. The repair bill was estimated at £60 billion.

Volcanoes

In September 2000 Mount Oyama erupted again, forcing residents to flee. Smoke rose as high as 3000 metres. Experts said it was the highest level of activity recently observed from the 813-metre high volcano. About 630 people were ordered to evacuate the Tsubota and Kamitsuki areas. Here, a man tries to clean ash off his car.

Floods and landslides

In 1997 heavy rains triggered 200 mudslides. The village of Izumi was hardest hit. Here, 80 families lived in a valley known to be vulnerable to landslides. The government recognised the threat and started to build a 16-metre high concrete barrier. But it proved to be no protection. At 1 am on 16 July an avalanche of bright red mud, boulders and trees roared down the hill, crashing right through the barrier.

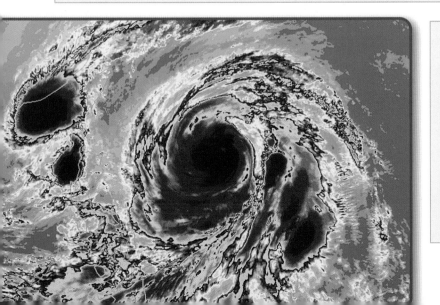

Typhoons

Typhoons (left) develop in warm tropical waters and have winds of at least 65 kph. An average of 28 typhoons form between June and September each year, but usually only two or three pass across Japan. There have been few disasters recently because of improved forecasting techniques and better methods of warning people. The worst recent typhoon killed 19 people in September 1991.

Case Study

What do we learn about Japan from the media?

Word	How to draw/write	Kanji
Paddy field	𠆢 冂 冊 用 田	田
Tree	一 十 才 木	木 木木 (Woods) 森 (Forest)
Mountain	卜 山 山	山
River	丿 刂刂 川	川

A Japanese kanji

A major difference between Japan, China and western countries is the style of writing. Japanese writing developed from the Chinese system and in both systems the symbols represent something. The symbolic parts of the writing are called **kanji**. Diagram **A** shows how some of these symbols have come about, and how to draw them. It is important to follow the arrows as these have been developed to ensure legible handwriting!

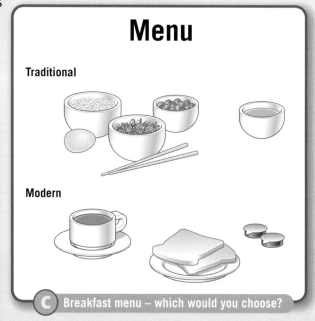

Menu

Traditional

Modern

C Breakfast menu – which would you choose?

'Rice' and 'food' mean almost the same thing in Japan. Breakfast is literally translated as 'morning rice', while lunch would be 'noon rice' and dinner 'evening rice'. But like many other aspects of Japanese life, attitudes are changing. Few young people would choose the traditional breakfast menu from diagram **C** nowadays.

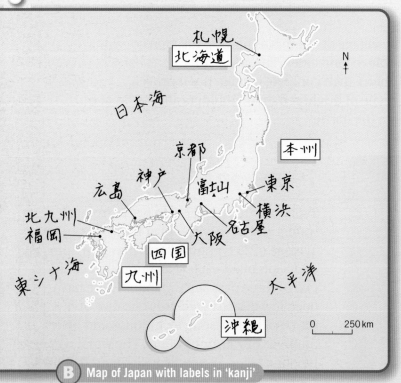

B Map of Japan with labels in 'kanji'

Japan was cut off from the rest of the world until the mid-nineteenth century. When contact was at last made, the people of Europe and America often treated the Japanese people as oriental curiosities and within a very short space of time the Japanese were described as 'naïve children' and 'inscrutable'.

Japanese art and culture, as well as the unfamiliar religious philosophies such as Shintō and Buddhism, seemed strange and mysterious. The overall western attitude was often prejudiced and based upon stereotypes. In recent years Japan has become very good at turning these negative images into positive ones. Many business managers around the world have studied Japanese management techniques. Zen meditation and Buddhism have many converts. The Japanese language is taught in an increasing number of UK schools.

D Traditional Japanese art

E Urban living

F Traditional Japanese sword play demonstration

Activities

1 a Make a sketch map of a small, imaginary Japanese island. Label it using some of the kanji symbols in diagram **A**.

  b How easy did you find it to write the kanji? Why do you think this is?

2 Study photographs **D**, **E** and **F**. Stereotypes are bad because they are based on biased and incomplete information.

  a List the ways in which the information in the photographs is incomplete.

  b What photographs would you take to balance these pictures to make the image complete? Look through the pictures of Japan in this unit to help you with ideas.

3 **Extension**

  How would you set about challenging stereotypes about Japan? (Pages 108 and 109 may give you some ideas.)

Trading places?

On 19 May 2000 China joined the World Trade Organisation (photograph **A**). The central issue that had to be resolved before China could join the WTO was how European companies would be allowed access to the mobile phone market in China.

Trade is vital to both China and Japan's economic success. China's success as one of the world's largest trading nations is all the more remarkable because it has achieved this since 1978 when the '**open policy**' was declared. By 1997 China and Japan were each other's largest trading partner (diagram **B**), and both countries have economic links with the rest of the world.

But while China's economy has gone from strength to strength, Japan has suffered a 'slow down' in economic growth in the past ten years. In April 2000 the value of Japanese industries was lower than it had been in 1985. Consumers are spending less money, so to maintain any economic growth Japan has to trade with other countries. The result has been an increase in trade, investment and aid with China.

A China joins the World Trade Organisation

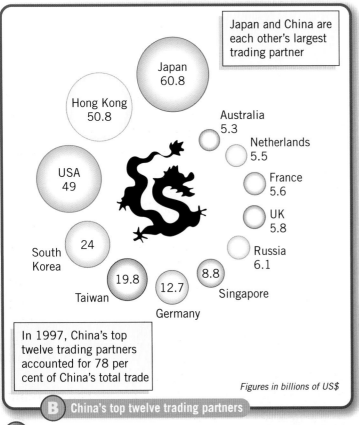

Japan and China are each other's largest trading partner

Japan 60.8

Hong Kong 50.8

Australia 5.3

Netherlands 5.5

USA 49

France 5.6

UK 5.8

24
South Korea

Russia 6.1

19.8
Taiwan

12.7
Germany

8.8
Singapore

In 1997, China's top twelve trading partners accounted for 78 per cent of China's total trade

Figures in billions of US$

B China's top twelve trading partners

Getting Technical ▼

- **Exports** are goods or services that are sent out or sold to another country.

- **Invisible exports** are payments for services, for example transport, shipping, banking and tourism.

- **Visible exports** include items such as foodstuffs, raw materials and manufactured goods.

- **Imports** are goods and services that are brought in from another country through trade.

- **Balance of trade** is the difference in value between exports and imports. When a country exports more goods and services than it imports, it has a **trade surplus.**

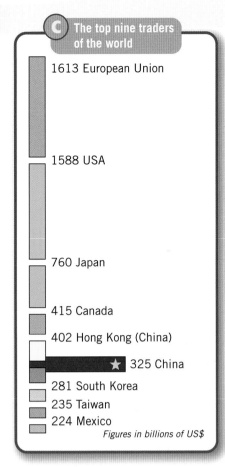

C The top nine traders of the world

1613 European Union

1588 USA

760 Japan

415 Canada

402 Hong Kong (China)

★ 325 China

281 South Korea

235 Taiwan

224 Mexico

Figures in billions of US$

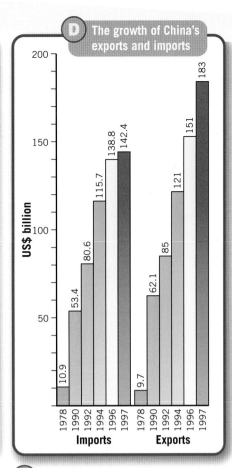

D The growth of China's exports and imports

US$ billion

Imports

10.9 (1978)
53.4 (1990)
80.6 (1992)
115.7 (1994)
138.8 (1996)
142.4 (1997)

Exports

9.7 (1978)
62.1 (1990)
85 (1992)
121 (1994)
151 (1996)
183 (1997)

Activities

1 Study graph **D**.

  a Work out the balance of trade between China and the rest of the world for each year.

  b Write a sentence to describe what changes in trade the graph shows. The text on page 106 will help you explain what the graph tells you about China's economy.

2 Since when has China had a trade surplus? What do you think China should spend this surplus on?

3 Study the information about Hong Kong here and on page 99. Write a short summary (no more than 30 words) to explain why Hong Kong is an important trading centre.

Hong Kong, a special administrative region

Hong Kong grew originally because it was on a trade route and had a large, deep, sheltered harbour. It became part of China in 1997. The city is one of the world's most prosperous economies, and the population is growing rapidly. It is estimated that the number of people will increase from 6.7 million in 1999 to 8.2 million by 2015. Hong Kong is in the right place geographically and it is one of the main ports to import goods into mainland China. A new airport was recently built on Lantau island, which is linked to the mainland by road and rail bridges. A map to show the location of Hong Kong can be found on page 99.

E Hong Kong

What links do China and Japan have with the UK?

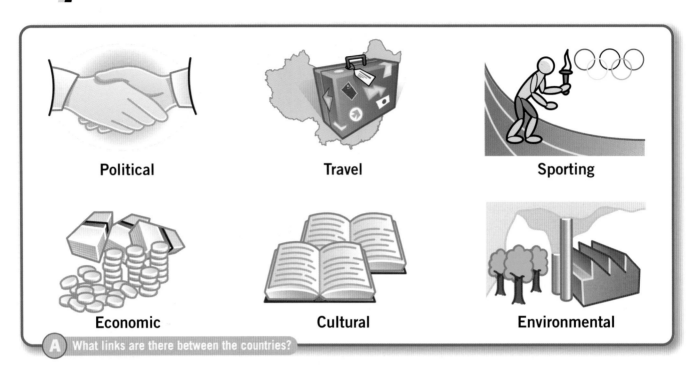

Political

Travel

Sporting

Economic

Cultural

Environmental

A What links are there between the countries?

Japan has a long history of economic links with the UK. The UK is Japan's main trading partner in Europe, and many Japanese companies have invested in factories in the UK (diagram **B** and photograph **C**). Between 1997 and 2001 the Japanese economy grew very little. However, the Chinese economy continues to thrive and in March 2001 it was growing at a rate of 8 per cent. Chinese exports were up by 28 per cent in 2000 and Chinese imports rose by 35 per cent.

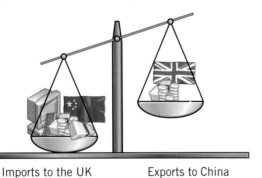

Imports to the UK
from China in 2000
£5 005 million

Exports to China
from the UK in 2000
£1 468 million

Imports to the UK
from Japan in 1999
£9 251 million

Exports to Japan
from the UK in 1999
£3 303 million

B Trade links between China, Japan and the UK

C Japanese investment in high-tech factories in the UK (Mitsubishi, Scotland)

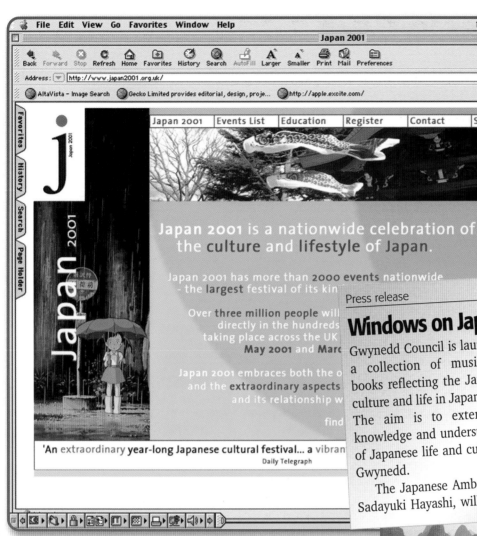

Japan 2001 is a nationwide celebration of the culture and lifestyle of Japan. Over two million people will participate in the hundreds of events taking place across the UK between May 2001 and March 2002. Japan 2001 celebrates both the ordinary and the extraordinary aspects of Japan and its relationship with the UK.

Press release

5 June 2001

Windows on Japan

Gwynedd Council is launching a collection of music and books reflecting the Japanese culture and life in Japan today. The aim is to extend the knowledge and understanding of Japanese life and culture in Gwynedd.

The Japanese Ambassador, Sadayuki Hayashi, will launch the collection at Bangor Library on Saturday 9 June. The collection will tour Gwynedd's main libraries during the year.

Gwynedd Council has been working with the staff of the Institute of Japanese Studies, University of Wales, Bangor on this venture.

D Cultural links between Japan and the UK

E Travel links between China and the UK

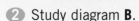

Activities

1 Study box **D**, which shows some of the cultural links between the UK and Japan.

a What are cultural links?

b Why do you think Gwynedd Council in North Wales has set up the collection of books and music?

c What do you think the Japan 2001 series of cultural events hope to achieve? Why are events such as these important?

d i Choose one other type of link shown in diagram **A** and make a list of the activities and events that could be organised to strengthen this link.

ii How would Japan and the UK benefit from these activities?

2 Study diagram **B**.

a Work out the balance of trade between the UK and China and the UK and Japan.

b If the economy of Japan is not growing and the economy of China is growing, what would your economic forecast be for the way in which imports and exports from the UK to these countries will change?

c Do you think Chinese factories similar to the Japanese one in photograph **C** will be built in the UK? Explain your answer.

Review and reflect

Activities

1 Look back at the list of ten questions you wrote down for question **1c** on page 89.

   a Have you found answers to them all?

   b Now you know more about Japan and China, would you like to change any of your questions? If so, which questions would you ask instead?

   c What sort of information was the hardest to find?

2 Look back at the photographs on pages 88–89. The captions to the photographs are listed here. How do they compare with the captions you wrote?

C Great Wall of China

D Beijing centre

E Farmer in Nagano-ken, Japan

F Main road in Tokyo

G Japan NKK steelworks

H Volkswagen car plant, Shanghai, China

3 Now you have collected your information, you can start to plan your report to compare Japan and China. Diagram **A** reminds you about the steps you need to take when carrying out a geographical enquiry.

You need to present your findings in the form of a report. There are many ways of doing this, not all of them written. Diagram **B** shows some ideas.

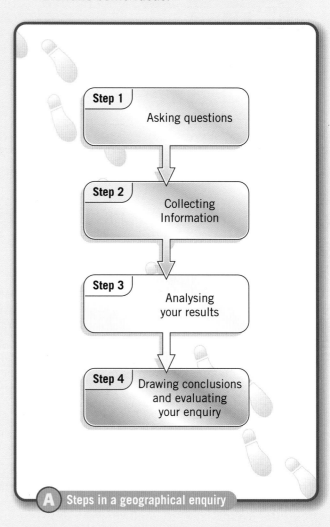

Step 1 Asking questions

Step 2 Collecting Information

Step 3 Analysing your results

Step 4 Drawing conclusions and evaluating your enquiry

A Steps in a geographical enquiry

B Reporting back

Written report

Spoken report

Microsoft PowerPoint presentation

Published on a website

Wall display

Radio documentary

Series of posters

How to ...

If you decide to present a written report, you might like to follow this structure:

- *Introduction to set the scene* – What have you studied? What questions did you ask? Explain the focus of your report. Where are China and Japan? Define the terms you will use, e.g. economic development.

- *Data collection* – What data have you collected? How and where did you collect the data? How reliable is the data?

- *Analysis and explanation* – This is the most important section. Use as many ways to illustrate your data as possible, e.g. maps, diagrams, photographs, graphs, tables, charts and written paragraphs. Make sure you answer the questions you outlined in your introduction.

- *Conclusion and evaluation* – Look back at the focus of your report, which was to compare two countries at different stages of economic development. Use the things you have learned about as guidance, and write a summary paragraph for each one in your conclusion. Remember to evaluate what you have done, e.g. which parts of your enquiry went well, and which parts could have been improved.

- *List of sources (bibliography)* – Include a list of all the sources of data you used. Set them out like this:

  Book, article or website author; title; publisher; date of publication.

6 Tourism – good or bad?

What is tourism?

Learn about

People in most parts of the developed world now have more holidays than ever before. Travel and tourism make up the world's largest group of industries. In this unit you will learn:

- the different types of holidays people can take
- what jobs are provided by the tourism industry
- how important the tourism industry is to some countries
- how the tourism industry is changing
- how the impact of visitors on the places they visit can be positive or negative
- how tourism can be more sustainable.

How important is tourism as an economic activity?

Fact file: Tourism

- Tourism employs more people than any other industry in the world.
- Income from international tourism was US $476 billion in 2000.
- More tourists (75.5 million) visited France than any other country in 2000.
- The USA received US $85.2 billion from tourism in 2000 – more than any other country.

Activities

1. **a** With a partner, look at photographs **A** to **G** and make a list of all the different types of holiday they show. Add as many others as you can think of.

   b How many different groups or headings can you fit those types of holiday in to?

2. **a** For each photograph, make a list of all the attractions of that area.

   b Identify whether these attractions are physical/natural (e.g. snow in photograph **E**), or human (e.g. the Eiffel Tower in photograph **B**).

3. Choose one photograph of a place you would like to visit. Can you think of any negative impacts people might have on the area in the photograph you have chosen?

4. Look at all the photographs on page 112. List all the jobs that will be created by the types of holidays that you can see. Start from the moment they are advertised on TV. Classify the jobs according to their type, as shown in the table below.

Primary sector jobs	Secondary sector jobs	Tertiary sector jobs
Farmers to supply food to hotels	Construction worker at hotel	Travel agent

5. Shade all the jobs which you think will be seasonal, i.e. only available at certain times of the year. Explain why this is the case.

6. Copy and complete a large version of the Venn diagram on the right by writing each job in the correct section.

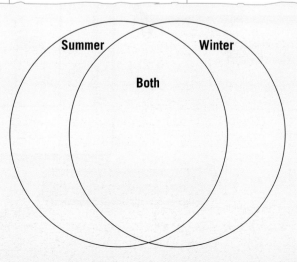

How and why is the tourism industry changing?

Tourism is a constantly changing industry. Many things influence where people choose to go on holiday. For example, some people like to go to familiar places, others are looking for somewhere different. There are also fashions for different types of holidays and, of course, for most people price is important. Many holiday resorts have gone through a period of growth followed by a period of decline as people change their choice of holiday. The graphs and tables on these pages show some of the changing patterns of holidays taken by people from the UK and some reasons for those patterns.

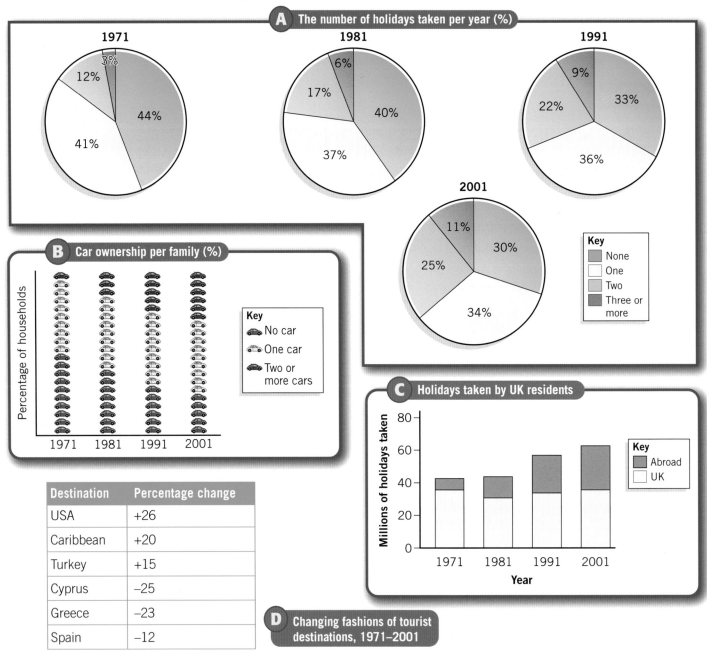

A The number of holidays taken per year (%)

1971
3%
12%
44%
41%

1981
6%
17%
40%
37%

1991
9%
33%
22%
36%

2001
11%
30%
25%
34%

Key
- None
- One
- Two
- Three or more

B Car ownership per family (%)

Percentage of households

1971　1981　1991　2001

Key
- No car
- One car
- Two or more cars

C Holidays taken by UK residents

Millions of holidays taken

1971　1981　1991　2001
Year

Key
- Abroad
- UK

Destination	Percentage change
USA	+26
Caribbean	+20
Turkey	+15
Cyprus	−25
Greece	−23
Spain	−12

D Changing fashions of tourist destinations, 1971–2001

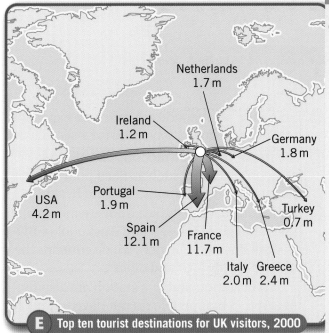

Netherlands
1.7 m

Ireland
1.2 m

Germany
1.8 m

USA
4.2 m

Portugal
1.9 m

Turkey
0.7 m

Spain
12.1 m

Italy Greece
2.0 m 2.4 m

France
11.7 m

E Top ten tourist destinations for UK visitors, 2000

Blackpool to Benidorm

- On the first post-war Saturday of July 1945, trains carried a record 102 890 trippers to Blackpool. Beaches had been off-limits since the start of the war.

- The Holiday with Pay Act turned this weekend exodus into a two-week annual adventure for workers.

- The working class went to Blackpool or Rothesay. The middle classes preferred the more select beaches of St Andrews and Troon.

- In the summer of 1948 there were almost 8000 cases of polio in Britain. Many were blamed on the polluted beaches around Britain's coast.

- In 1948 one in 20 British holidaymakers went to a Butlin's holiday camp for their holidays.

- By the 1960s millions of Britons were creating Rothesays and Musselboroughs on the Mediterranean Sea and in 1970 5.7 million British people chose to go to Spain on holiday, mostly through package tours.

- By 2000, 40 per cent of all holidays taken by Britons were spent abroad.

F Adapted from *The Guardian*, July 1999

Activities

1 Copy and complete the following paragraphs:

Since 1971 the number of holidays taken by residents of Great Britain has increased from _____ million to _____ million. An increasing proportion of these have been taken abroad and by 2001 _____ per cent of holidays were taken outside Great Britain.

Reasons for the increase in holidays might include the fact that more people own cars. In 1971 _____ million families had no car, but by 2001 this figure had decreased to _____ million. The increase in the number of motorways has also made resorts more accessible.

In 1971, 56 per cent of the population took at least one holiday. By 2001 this had risen to _____ per cent.

This is because _____ .

The introduction of the package holiday meant that it was easy to travel abroad, and in 2000 the three most popular holiday destinations for Britons were _____ , _____ and _____ .

2 Prepare a report for the British Tourist Authority on the main changes and trends in the tourism industry in the UK since 1971. Include sections on:
- the total demand for holidays
- the types of holidays people choose to go on
- the destinations of the holidaymakers
- how you think that the holiday industry may change in the future.

a Begin each section of the report with an enquiry question. For example, the first paragraph could start with: 'How has the demand for holidays changed and what are the reasons for this?'

b Include in your report graphs, diagrams, maps and pictures.

3 **Extension**
You may wish to make a database and generate your graphs using a computer. More information is available from tourism websites (see www.heinemann.co.uk/hotlinks for suggestions). ICT

Case Study

What is the impact of the tourist industry in Blackpool and St Lucia?

Blackpool

Blackpool is a typical British seaside resort. The coming of the railway in 1846 made Blackpool a busy, popular holiday destination as it was within an hour's ride of the dirty, smoky cotton towns of Manchester, Bolton and Rochdale. For many mill workers, the highlight of the year was the works' outing to Blackpool. The arrival of cars and coaches made Blackpool much more accessible to people from Scotland, especially Glaswegians during 'The Glesga Fair' (the local two-week summer holiday). Blackpool continued to grow, and today 16 million people visit the town each year.

- There are 11 km of wide sandy beach backed by a promenade where people like to walk.

- Lining the promenade are the more expensive hotels where guests pay more for a sea view.

- The major tourist attractions can also be found in this zone, such as Blackpool Tower, the piers and the famous Pleasure Beach.

- In the zone behind the sea front are the cheaper hotels and guest houses, and Blackpool's CBD (Central Business District), which contains the main shopping area and offices.

- The train station and bus station are also in this area so that people do not have to walk far to reach the beach or the other attractions.

- Furthest away from the sea are the residential areas, parks and other areas of commercial land use, such as the business park.

A

The Illuminations . . . .

First installed in 1879, the lights stretch for about nine kilometres along the sea front. They attract 8 million visitors a year and shine for 66 nights, extending the season by nine weeks at a time when most other resorts have closed down.

B Aerial view of Blackpool

Blackpool's heyday as a holiday destination for the British annual family holiday is long gone. The number of visitors staying and spending money in Blackpool has fallen in the past 30 years as people go abroad for better weather. People are changing not only their holiday destinations, but also the types of holidays they take. Far more holidaymakers camp, climb, visit rainforests and theme parks, or travel long distances than ever before.

The government has set up tourist boards in England, Wales, Scotland and Northern Ireland to give advice to businesses and to provide information for tourists. Resorts are encouraged to adapt to the changing demand for short breaks, day trips and special interest holidays, and cash for improvements is available from the National Lottery.

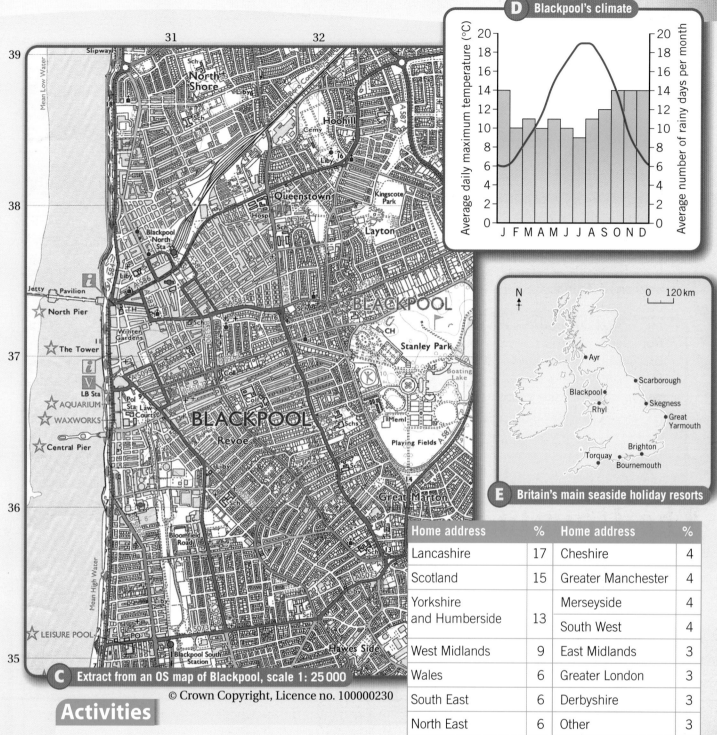

D Blackpool's climate

Average daily maximum temperature (°C) / Average number of rainy days per month

J F M A M J J A S O N D

E Britain's main seaside holiday resorts

N

0   120 km

Ayr

Scarborough

Blackpool

Skegness

Rhyl

Great Yarmouth

Brighton

Torquay

Bournemouth

C Extract from an OS map of Blackpool, scale 1:25 000

© Crown Copyright, Licence no. 100000230

Home address	%	Home address	%
Lancashire	17	Cheshire	4
Scotland	15	Greater Manchester	4
Yorkshire and Humberside	13	Merseyside	4
		South West	4
West Midlands	9	East Midlands	3
Wales	6	Greater London	3
South East	6	Derbyshire	3
North East	6	Other	3

F Home addresses of visitors to Blackpool, July 2000

Activities

1. Write a paragraph to explain why Blackpool has declined as a popular destination for holidaymakers.

2. Make a list of all the ways that Blackpool tries to extend its season to provide more work.

3. Use photograph **B** to draw a sketch map of the land use zones in Blackpool. Use map **C** to help you. Use one colour to label the natural attractions (for example, the sea) and another colour to label the human attractions (for example, the Tower).

4. You can find out more about Blackpool on the Internet. Visit www.heinemann.co.uk/hotlinks.

help!

Think about climate, attractions and alternative destinations.

St Lucia

St Lucia is an island of 616 km² in the Windward Islands chain, 160 km due west of Barbados. The capital city of Castries and the surrounding villages in the north are home to 40 per cent of the island's population and these are also the most popular tourist areas.

Until recently the main income for the islanders has come from growing and exporting bananas. Today, however, the island receives as much income from tourism as it does from the traditional cash crop. Although the St Lucians realise the importance of tourism to their country, they are working hard to avoid ruining their land with overbuilding. The island is also diversifying its agricultural base, which strengthens its economy further by reducing imports. Other cash crops include mangoes, tomatoes, limes and oranges.

A St Lucia, a tropical paradise

B The location of St Lucia

ANTIGUA
Puerto Rico
Guadeloupe
Atlantic Ocean
DOMINICA
Martinique
Caribbean Sea
ST LUCIA
ST VINCENT
BARBADOS
GRENADA
0   250 km
TRINIDAD
VENEZUELA

Castries
St Lucia's bustling capital is home to several of the island's historic sights. There is excellent shopping in the town's market.

Gros Islet
This village comes alive for the Friday night jazz street parties.

East coast
The east coast road twists and turns through many villages, passing many banana and coconut plantations.

Canaries
An afternoon's visit to this tiny fishing village offers an interesting study of one of St Lucia's main traditions – fishing in dugout canoes.

Rainforest
The central part of the island is covered in rainforest, where wild orchids, giant ferns and birds of paradise flourish, including the indigenous and rare St Lucia parrot.

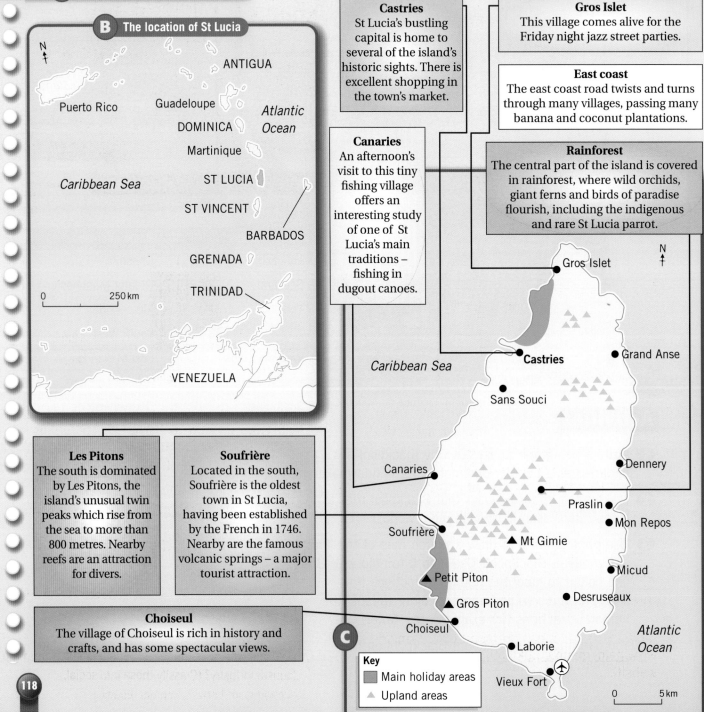

Gros Islet
Castries • Grand Anse
Caribbean Sea
Sans Souci
Canaries
Dennery
Soufrière
Praslin
Mon Repos
▲ Mt Gimie
▲ Petit Piton
Micud
▲ Gros Piton
Desruseaux
Choiseul
Laborie
Atlantic Ocean
Vieux Fort

Les Pitons
The south is dominated by Les Pitons, the island's unusual twin peaks which rise from the sea to more than 800 metres. Nearby reefs are an attraction for divers.

Soufrière
Located in the south, Soufrière is the oldest town in St Lucia, having been established by the French in 1746. Nearby are the famous volcanic springs – a major tourist attraction.

Choiseul
The village of Choiseul is rich in history and crafts, and has some spectacular views.

Key
▨ Main holiday areas
▲ Upland areas

0   5 km

C

❤ *Weddings and honeymoons in St Lucia*

St Lucia, known for its lush tropical beauty and breathtaking scenery, is highly regarded as a romantic treat and a honeymoon and wedding destination. Most of the hotels in St Lucia provide special facilities for couples getting married on the island; some will also provide a private room or suite for the ceremony, if you prefer.

D

ST LUCIA MIRROR

WATER SHORTAGE

Hotel owners warn that water rationing will affect trade.

E Adapted from a newspaper article

BRITISH FOREIGN OFFICE ADVICE TO VISITORS

Last Updated: 11 May 2001

Most visits to St Lucia are trouble-free, but visitors should be aware that crime is on the increase and muggings can occur at any time, day or night. Visitors should not become complacent because of the friendly, laid-back nature of the island.

F Advice to visitors

Average number of rainy days per month	Month	Average maximum daily temperature (°C)
18	January	28
13	February	28
13	March	29
10	April	31
16	May	31
21	June	31
23	July	31
22	August	31
21	September	31
19	October	31
20	November	29
19	December	28

G St Lucia's climate

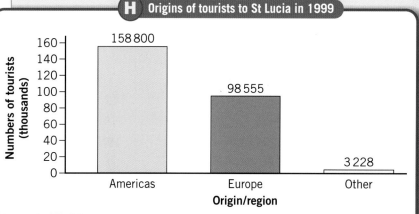

H Origins of tourists to St Lucia in 1999

(Bar chart: Numbers of tourists (thousands) by Origin/region — Americas: 158 800, Europe: 98 555, Other: 3 228)

Activities

1 Draw a sketch map of St Lucia and annotate it with the attractions of the island for a holidaymaker. Use one colour to label the natural attractions (for example, Les Pitons) and another colour to label the human attractions (for example, the market at Castries).

2 Use table **G** to draw a climate graph for St Lucia. (123)

3 Choose either Blackpool or St Lucia and carry out an enquiry to answer the following question:

> Is Blackpool/St Lucia a successful tourist destination?

a More information can be found by clicking on www.heinemann.co.uk/hotlinks for St Lucia websites.

b Write up your work as a poster which can be displayed to show the good and bad points of tourism in your chosen resort. You could use a desktop publishing program to produce this. (ICT)

4 Write a five-minute script for a television holiday programme which compares Blackpool and St Lucia. Use the following headings:

⊚ What is the resort like?

⊚ What does it offer visitors? (Think about natural and human attractions.)

⊚ Who goes there and where are they from?

⊚ How and why does the resort benefit or suffer from the tourism industry? (Classify these into social, economic and environmental effects.)

How can tourism be more sustainable?

Many developing countries are becoming popular tourist destinations. Tourism can bring many benefits, such as jobs. It can also result in costs, such as pollution or environmental damage. People in these countries are also made more aware of the inequalities between themselves and the visitors in terms of their quality of life. Visitors can sometimes offend the local people by the way they dress or the lack of respect they show for local customs and religion.

The key is to minimise the damage – to strike a balance so that holidaymakers can enjoy themselves without destroying what attracted them in the first place. This type of tourism is known as **sustainable tourism** or **ecotourism** and is relevant to all places, whether they are seaside resorts, urban areas or countryside in developing or developed countries. Sustainable tourism also means making sure that local people benefit from the industry, not just big tour companies. For example, local people need to be involved in making decisions which affect their lives.

How to be an ecotourist

Before you go
- Get rid of unnecessary packaging and swap plastic for paper.
- Try to take eco-friendly shampoos and sun lotions.

While you're away
- Get out and be adventurous – if you always stay in the hotel, little money will filter through to local people.
- Try local dishes and drinks instead of sticking to imported brands.

In the hotel
- Don't waste energy. Turn off the lights and air-conditioning when you leave your room.
- Don't waste water.

A Adapted from an extract in *Holiday Which?*, Spring 1999

Out and about
- Consider using public transport or hire a bicycle to get around.
- Buy presents and souvenirs from local craftspeople and pay a fair price.
- Ask permission before photographing people.
- Dress appropriately – don't offend local people. Remember you are a guest in their country.

Activities

1. Write a sentence to explain what is meant by sustainable tourism.

2. Copy and complete the table to show how five suggestions in box **A** encourage sustainable tourism. One example has been completed for you.

Suggestion	Reason(s)
Get rid of unnecessary packaging	Host country does not have to burn or bury additional waste

Review and reflect

What are the effects of tourism?

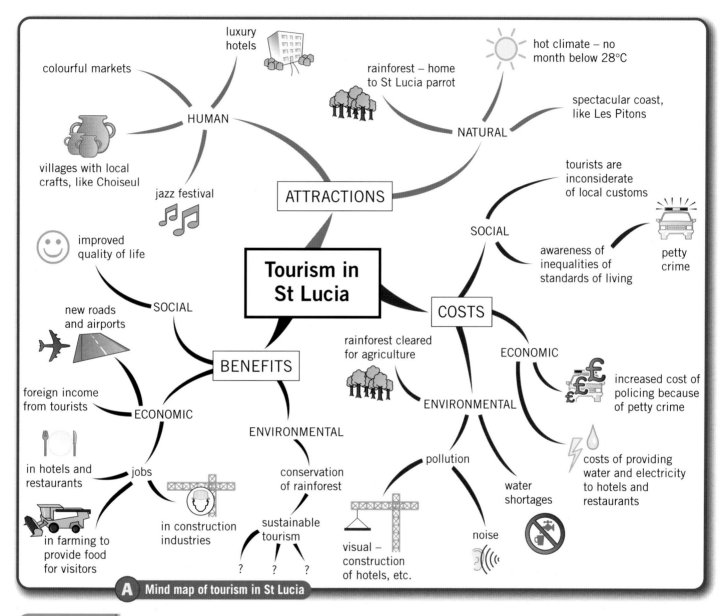

A Mind map of tourism in St Lucia

Activities

1 a Look carefully at the mind map above. It shows information about the tourism industry in St Lucia – an economically less developed country. Use it as a model to draw a similar mind map for a holiday resort in the United Kingdom, or another more economically developed country of your choice.

  b Collect some holiday brochures and use information from pages 113 to 120 here to help investigate them. If you are able to, add facts from research you have carried out on the Internet. **ICT**

  c Try to expand your mind map to include ways in which tourism at your chosen resort could become more sustainable.

2 Add the key words from this unit to your word bank. 📖

7 Cars on the Internet

The global car industry

Making cars is one of the world's growth industries. In 2000, sales for passenger cars around the world rose to 49.4 million, the highest ever. The demand for all vehicles, including trucks and vans, increased to 58.2 million. As graph **A** shows, sales of new cars have grown steadily over the past twenty years. However, car sales and production are unevenly distributed around the world (table **B** and map **C**).

A World car sales, 1983–2000

*Source: *The World's Car Manufacturers, Edition 4*

Region	Number of new cars sold
USA, Canada and Mexico	19 770 000
South America	1 922 000
Western Europe	15 120 000
Eastern Europe	2 592 000
Middle East	1 017 000
Africa	619 000
Japan	4 230 000
Asia except Japan	3 520 000
Australia/New Zealand	645 000
World	**49 435 000**

B New car sales, 2000

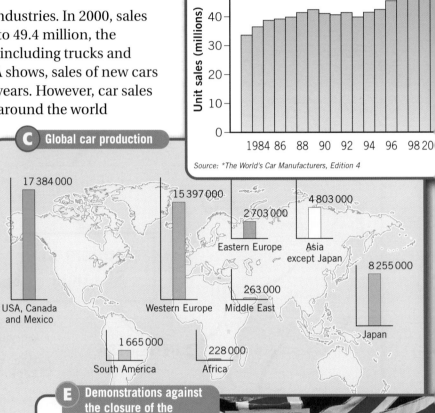

C Global car production

17 384 000 — USA, Canada and Mexico
15 397 000 — Western Europe
2 703 000 — Eastern Europe
4 803 000 — Asia except Japan
263 000 — Middle East
8 255 000 — Japan
1 665 000 — South America
228 000 — Africa

D Launch of the new Mini

E Demonstrations against the closure of the Longbridge plant in 2000

DON'T LET ROVER DIE

F Using technology to make cars

Learn about

In this unit you will learn about:

◉ the global car industry

◉ changes in the car industry in the UK

◉ BMW, a global car producer

◉ the car industry in Europe.

You will use the Internet to gain information on the car industry, to find out people's opinions on changes in the car industry, and as a way of communicating your findings and feelings to fellow pupils.

Activities

1 In pairs, discuss graph **A** and photographs **D–F**. What do they tell you about changes in the car industry? Share your ideas before making a list of the changes.

2 Use the data in table **B** to draw located bars showing new car sales on a world map. You will need a base outline map of the world. (123)

3 a Describe the pattern of global car production shown on map **C**.

b Compare car manufacturing (map **C**) with the map you have drawn to show car sales.

c Explain your findings. For example:

  ⑥ suggest reasons why some regions have high or low sales

  ⑥ suggest reasons why some regions make many or few cars.

Research activity (ICT)

4 Use the Internet to investigate the global car industry.

a As with any other sort of enquiry, good geographers start by asking questions. Work in pairs to think of the questions you might want to ask about the car industry. Use the Six Ws to help you: **W**hat? **W**here? **W**ho? **W**hen? **W**hy? Ho**W**? and aim to list two or more questions for each. For example:

  ⑥ Where are cars produced?

  ⑥ What changes are occurring?

b Visit the auto industry website through www.heinemann.co.uk/hotlinks. This site includes data on car production for the UK, Europe and the world. To find out about world car production, click on the World icon once you have opened the website.

c Choose one or two key pieces of information from the website which help to answer each of your questions. When you present them, remember to say what the information tells you.

d Which questions turned out to be difficult to answer from the website?

How to ...

... draw located bar charts

1 Map **C** shows you how to draw located bars.

2 Use a similar scale for your map of car sales. Try a scale of 2 mm = 1 million new cars sold.

help!

Good geographers look for key points when describing and explaining global patterns. Clever geographers make it sound easy! For example, consider:

❂ which regions are the largest producers?

❂ which regions are the less important producers?

❂ are most of the producers MEDCs or LEDCs?

❂ are they in the northern hemisphere (north of the Equator) or in the southern hemisphere (south of the Equator)?

❂ are there any exceptions?

The UK car industry

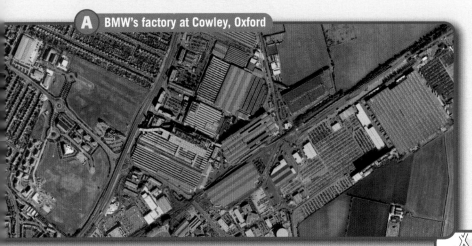

A | BMW's factory at Cowley, Oxford

Most car **manufacturers** look for a number of **factors** when they are building a new factory. These include:

- a large area of cheap, flat land
- good **communications**
- a reliable and skilled workforce
- a nearby **market** for selling cars
- supporting industries that make **components**.

The UK's car industry is very important to the country's economy. About 790 000 jobs depend on it, including about 330 000 workers directly employed in making vehicles and components. The UK has over twenty motor vehicle manufacturers, but six **multinational companies** produce almost three-quarters of all cars. They are:

- Ford (including Jaguar and Land Rover)
- Vauxhall (owned by General Motors)
- Peugeot
- Honda
- Nissan
- Toyota.

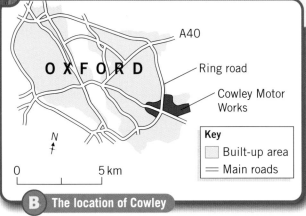

B | The location of Cowley

C | The new Mini assembly line

Changes in jobs

The car industry changes rapidly. Since the 1960s many UK car firms have been taken over by rival firms and some have gone out of business altogether. For example, in 2000 BMW sold Rover and Land Rover, and in 2001 Ford stopped producing the Escort at its Dagenham plant. These changes affect many people and other businesses. For example, the car works at Cowley in Oxford employed over 25 000 workers in the 1970s. By 2000 it employed just 2500 workers. But in 2001 production of the new Mini created more than 1000 extra jobs (photographs **A** and **C**).

Despite these changes, many companies still make cars and commercial vehicles in the UK. As shown on map **D**, many of them are specialist firms. As well as car manufacturers, over 1250 other companies make car components, and more than 100 000 people work in the car components industry, which makes £8 billion a year.

Changes in car production

More and more new cars are being made and sold. In the UK in 1999:

⑥ new car registrations reached 2.2 million, the fourth highest figure on record

⑥ sales of cars were worth more than £31 billion

⑥ car production reached its highest level since 1972, but the manufacture of vans, lorries and coaches declined.

As well as changes in the number of cars produced, car manufacturers sell increasing numbers of cars abroad as **exports**. More than 1.1 million passenger cars were produced for export in 1999 – more than three times the exports in 1990.

Changes in investment

When a car company wants to build a new car, it needs to **invest** money in new designs, new equipment, and sometimes new factories. These are very expensive. Since the late 1970s Japanese and American car companies have invested huge sums of money in the European car industry, much of it in the UK. Since 1997, companies have invested over £3 billion in the UK car industry, creating approximately 9700 jobs.

D Car production in the UK, 2000

Number on map	Company	Location	Number of cars produced
1	Nissan	Sunderland	271 157
2	Ford	Dagenham	190 970
3	Vauxhall	Luton	184 243
4	Toyota	Burnaston	178 660
5	BMW	Longbridge	172 099
6	Vauxhall	Ellesmere Port	168 035
7	Land Rover (BMW)	Solihull	166 101
8	Peugeot	Coventry	162 921
9	Ford	Halewood	115 479
10	Honda	Swindon	114 479
11	Jaguar/Daimler (Ford)	Coventry	86 317
12	Ford	Southampton	66 814
13	BMW	Cowley	53 673
14	Leyland Trucks	Leyland	8 115
15	Lotus	Norwich	3 374
16	London Taxis International	Coventry	3 142
17	TVR	Blackpool	1 460
18	Rolls Royce/Bentley	Crewe	1 440
19	Metrocab	Tamworth	624
20	Aston Martin	Banbury	565
21	Aston Martin	Newport Pagnell	57

Activities

① Study photograph **A**, which shows the BMW's factory at Cowley. Draw a sketch of the site and label the features that help describe and explain its location. Use the list of factors to help you.

② Use a large copy of map **D** to help you investigate the distribution of the UK car industry.

   a Use different colours to highlight:

   ⑥ mass-production factories (over 100 000 vehicles)

   ⑥ medium-sized factories (10 000 – 100 000 vehicles)

   ⑥ small specialist factories (under 10 000 vehicles).

   b Use symbols to identify the factories owned by multinational companies.

   c Add labels to your map, or write a short paragraph describing the distribution of car factories, then explain your findings.

③ Study the data in map **D** and read the text again. Why is the closure of car factories so important to the local and the national economy?

Research activity ICT

④ The Internet is a useful way for geographers to collect data. It is easy to find information from a range of sources, including newspapers, governments, companies and pressure groups.

Remember: some information on the Internet is unreliable or wrong. It might be biased in favour of the people who produced it.

Visit the website for the statistics section of the UK auto industry using

www.heinemann.co.uk/hotlinks.

Search for data on the world's largest vehicle manufacturers.

a How many of the world's top ten largest manufacturers belong to the UK?

b Which country has the most companies in the world's largest car companies?

c What changes in UK car production can you identify?

Case Study

Cowley

Rover fact file

- 1904: First Rover car produced.
- 1994: Rover bought by BMW, who paid £800 million.
- Brands – Rover, Land Rover, Range Rover, Mini and MG.
- Main UK factories at Longbridge, Solihull, Cowley and Swindon.
- 1999: Employed 37 000 people, with 50 000 jobs at firms supplying Rover.
- 1999: UK sales ranked sixth behind Ford, Vauxhall, Peugeot, Renault and Volkswagen.
- 1994–2000: Rover lost £550 million, with sales down 45 per cent.
- 2000: BMW sold Rover, MG and Land Rover.
- 2001: Production of the new BMW Mini began at its Cowley factory.

Back to the future for Cowley

The Cowley factory was closed in 2000 while BMW invested £230 million in new machinery and facilities to produce the 'Car of the Century' – the new Mini – there. For almost a year the workforce was retrained by visiting BMW factories in Germany and USA. Mass production of the new car at Cowley began in April 2001. BMW's plan is to produce 30 000 Minis in 2001, rising to 100 000 a year.

C Retail developments on the Cowley Works

BMW at Cowley

In 2000 BMW sold its Longbridge and Solihull factories but decided to keep the Cowley Works to produce the new Mini there. The Cowley Works is now more **automated** than it was in the 1970s and uses robots rather than people. Employment declined from 25 000 at the factory's peak in the 1970s to 2500 in 2000. Maps **A** and **B** show that even the size of the factory **site** has declined. Land has been sold off for an out-of-town shopping centre (photo **C**), a new business park (photo **D**), and new housing. Because of its good location next to a dual carriageway and on the edge of town, it has proved popular with the developers.

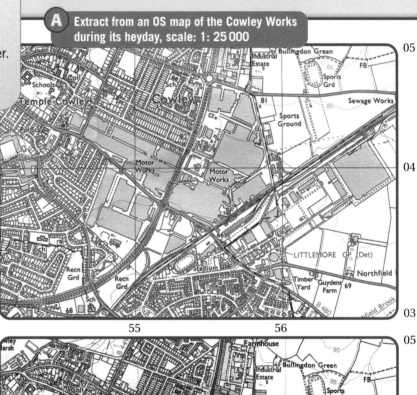

A Extract from an OS map of the Cowley Works during its heyday, scale: 1: 25 000

B Extract from an OS map of the Cowley Works in 2001, scale 1: 25 000

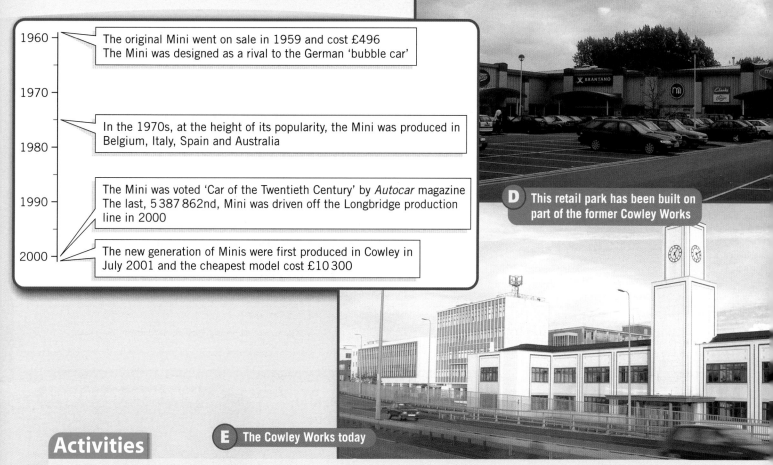

1960 — The original Mini went on sale in 1959 and cost £496
The Mini was designed as a rival to the German 'bubble car'

1970 —

1980 — In the 1970s, at the height of its popularity, the Mini was produced in Belgium, Italy, Spain and Australia

1990 — The Mini was voted 'Car of the Twentieth Century' by *Autocar* magazine
The last, 5 387 862nd, Mini was driven off the Longbridge production line in 2000

2000 — The new generation of Minis were first produced in Cowley in July 2001 and the cheapest model cost £10 300

D This retail park has been built on part of the former Cowley Works

E The Cowley Works today

Activities

1 Study maps **A** and **B**.

a Find map evidence that the Cowley factory has become less important. List the evidence or make a sketch map and add labels around it.

b With a partner, discuss the effects of this decline on local people and businesses, and on the local environment. Remember there may be positive as well as negative effects.

c Make notes from your discussion using a copy of the table below to help you:

	Positive effects	Negative effects
On people		
On businesses		
On the environment		

d Write a short paragraph explaining who or what you think are the winners and losers from the changes at Cowley.

2 Study photograph **D**.

a What kinds of businesses would you expect to find in a building like this?

b How does the site differ from the Cowley factory (photograph **E**)?

Research activity (ICT)

3 a Study an on-line map of the Oxford area from the Oxford City website through www.heinemann.co.uk/hotlinks

b Compare the information on this map with maps **A** and **B**. How useful is the on-line map? Give reasons to support your answer.

c What map evidence is there to suggest that the location of the site is a good one for developers?

d Investigate and compare maps of Oxford from other websites such as Ordnance Survey or Map Blast! at www.heinemann.co.uk/hotlinks

4 a Investigate BMW's UK website using the Heinemann web address to see what you can find out about the Mini.

b Click on the icon for Heritage, and find out when BMW was started, by whom, and what the company produced.

c Make a timeline for BMW, similar to the timeline above for the Mini.

Case Study

BMW – a European and global car manufacturer

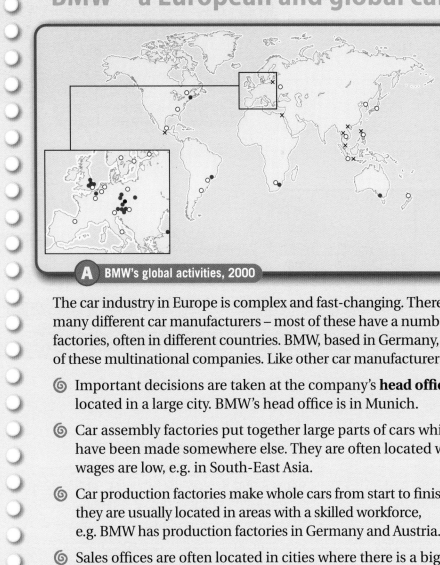

Key
- Munich Headquarters
- Production
- × Assembly plants
- ○ Sales and distribution locations

● Production
Berlin Plant
Birmingham Plant, UK
Dingolfing Plant
Eisenach Plant
Harms Hall Plant, UK
Landshut Plant
Munich Plant
Oxford Plant, UK
Regensburg Plant
Rosslyn Plant, South Africa
Spartanburg Plant, USA
Steyr Plant, Austria
Swindon Plant, UK
Tritec Motors Ltda, Curitiba, Brazil
Wackersdoft Plant

× Assembly plants
Toluca Plant, Mexico
Arnata City Plant, Thailand
CKD Production Cairo, Egypt
CKD Production Jakarta, Indonesia
CKD Production Kuala Lumpur, Malaysia
CKD Production Manila, Philippines
CKD Production Kaliningrad, Russia
CKD Production Hanoi, Vietnam

○ Sales and distribution locations

Argentina	Italy	Sweden
Australia	Japan	Switzerland
Austria	Mexico	Thailand
Belgium	New Zealand	USA
Brazil	Netherlands	
Canada	Norway	
Finland	Philippines	
France	Russia	
Germany	South Africa	
United Kingdom	South Korea	
Indonesia	Spain	

A BMW's global activities, 2000

The car industry in Europe is complex and fast-changing. There are many different car manufacturers – most of these have a number of factories, often in different countries. BMW, based in Germany, is one of these multinational companies. Like other car manufacturers:

- Important decisions are taken at the company's **head office** located in a large city. BMW's head office is in Munich.

- Car assembly factories put together large parts of cars which have been made somewhere else. They are often located where wages are low, e.g. in South-East Asia.

- Car production factories make whole cars from start to finish, so they are usually located in areas with a skilled workforce, e.g. BMW has production factories in Germany and Austria.

- Sales offices are often located in cities where there is a big enough market of wealthy people to buy the cars.

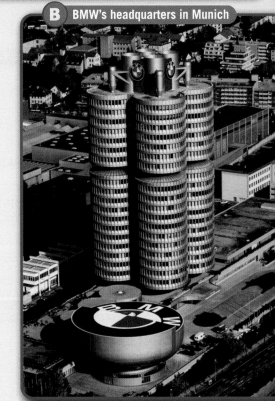

B BMW's headquarters in Munich

BMW's success

C The production factory in Spartanburg, USA

BMW is a highly successful company, with a reputation for making high-quality cars which are at the forefront of new technology. This image has helped make sure that year after year its sales continue to increase. As an example, in the USA General Motors and Ford sell many more vehicles, but BMW makes more than twice as much profit on each car it sells. BMW is not alone in its success. In Germany as a whole the car industry grew in the 1990s. For example, 75 000 new jobs were created between 1998 and 1999 and over DM700 million (£250 million) was invested in the industry in the years between 1995 and 2000. German car factories make 35 per cent of the total production in the European Union and 14 per cent in the world.

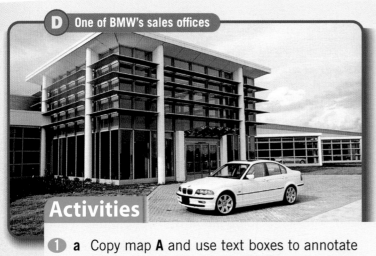

D One of BMW's sales offices

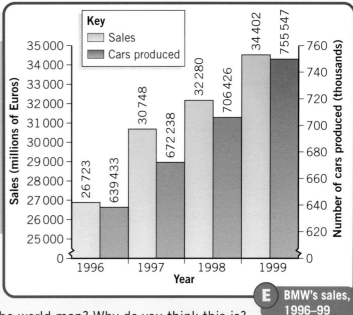

E BMW's sales, 1996–99

Activities

1 a Copy map **A** and use text boxes to annotate it. These notes should describe and explain the distribution of BMW's activities. **ICT**

  b Which of BMW's activities do not show up on the world map? Why do you think this is?

2 Study the information about BMW.

  a With a partner, discuss the effects of BMW's success for people and businesses in Munich, and on the local environment. Remember there may be positive as well as negative effects.

  b Make notes from your discussion using a copy of the table below to help you:

	Positive effects	Negative effects
On people		
On businesses		
On the environment		

  c Write a short paragraph explaining who or what you think are the winners and losers from the changes at BMW.

Research activity **ICT**

3 a Investigate other car manufacturers in Europe by searching the Internet. You could work in groups, with each group investigating a different company.

  b Find out the image of the company each website presents, and discuss what message it is trying to give to its customers.

  c Find out what the site tells you about changes in the company.

  d Compare the geographical information you have found out from each site – for example, where the company's activities are, and whether these are changing.

4 Extension

  a Investigate BMW's environmental policies using its website through using links in www.heinemann.co.uk/hotlinks. List the measures the company says it is taking to protect the environment.

  b Find a website for an environmental pressure group, such as Friends of the Earth. Investigate their views on transport issues, and especially the effects of cars. List the key points.

  c Compare the views of the car manufacturer and environmental groups, explaining any similarities and differences you have found.

help!
You might like to think about people and places outside Germany too.

Car production in Europe

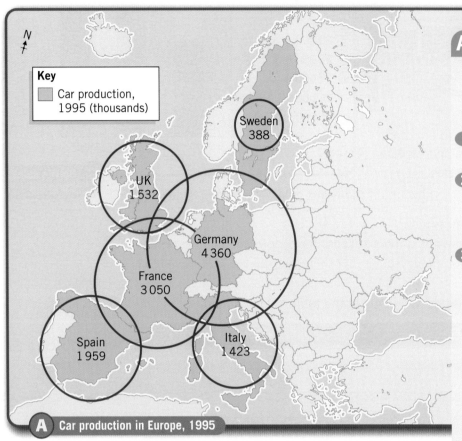

Key
Car production, 1995 (thousands)

Sweden 388

UK 1 532

Germany 4 360

France 3 050

Spain 1 959

Italy 1 423

A Car production in Europe, 1995

Map **A** shows car production in the mid 1990s. The research activity requires you to update it with current information.

1. Describe the pattern of car production shown in map **A**.

2. Suggest reasons why some European countries produce more cars than others.

Research activity ICT

3. As well as searching for information, geographers can collect information from the Internet and present it in a variety of forms, using word processing or spreadsheets, for example. But good geographers never copy directly – they always select information and adapt it to make it their own work.

   a Use the Internet to investigate car production in Europe, using one of these websites in
   www.heinemann.co.uk/hotlinks
   - UK Auto Industry statistics page, or
   - German Verband de Automobilindustrie.

   b Find out about changing car production in Europe, using these headings to help you:
   - the main car-producing countries
   - changes in car production in the past 5–10 years
   - the main car-manufacturing companies.

   c You could present your data by:
   - copying information into a spreadsheet, then using the program to sort the data and present it as charts
   - selecting useful text, copying it into a word processor, then editing it by using bullets and subheadings, and highlighting key points
   - using a presentation program to present your findings and your conclusions about change.

The market for cars in western Europe has grown from 13.4 million in 1997 to more than 15 million in 2000. At the same time, the market in North America has been booming. Wealthy consumers there are especially important for specialist European brands such as BMW, Mercedes and Porsche.

In spite of this, the car industry in western Europe is in crisis. A major problem is over-capacity. Car factories here are able to produce over 21 million cars a year, but in fact they sell only about 14.4 million cars a year. One solution is to cut costs by moving production to cheaper locations, for example Eastern Europe, where wages are lower. Another solution is global restructuring to try to cut costs. Many European car manufacturers have taken over, or been taken over by, multinational car companies. For example:

- Ford recently bought Land Rover and gained control of Volvo

- Daimler merged with Chrysler, then secured Mitsubishi.

Of course, these changes often have an impact on people, places and the environment near the car factories, as well as further away. Where there is economic change, there are usually winners and losers.

Review and reflect

Activities

1. You are familiar with finding answers to questions, especially geographical questions like the Six Ws: **W**hat? **W**here? **W**ho? **W**hen? **W**hy? Ho**W**? In pairs, look back over this unit and work out suitable questions to go with the answers below.

   a 58.2 million.

   b Car components.

   c Workers and other businesses at Cowley.

   d Workers and other businesses in Munich.

   e Mainly in Europe and North America.

   f Wages are lower there, so companies can make better profits.

   g General Motors.

   h A skilled workforce.

   i It might be biased or unreliable.

   j Robots do many tasks in the factory.

   help!

   Remember, some questions have only one answer, others can have several answers.

2. a Work out between five and ten of your own answers on the theme of the changing car industry. Try to make sure you have at least one for each of the Six Ws.

   b Test a partner to see if they can work out the questions to go with your answers.

3. Write a short report on the changing car industry and its effects, using the Six Ws to help you write headings. Use map **A** to help you write about the global car industry. If you use a word processing or presentation program to present your report, you could include hyperlinks to the most useful websites you have used in this unit. (ICT)

Key
- ○ Location
- ● Finished vehicles
- ◆ Parts sets
- ✛ Individual sets
- ■ CKD (completely knocked down) vehicles, i.e. the unassembled parts of one vehicle shipped together
- ★ Assemblies
- ▼ Spare parts

Map labels: VW Canada, VW America, VW Mexico, VW Japan, VW Shanghai, VW Nigeria, Autolatina Brazil, VW South Africa, Autolatina Argentina, VW Brussels, VW AG, Seat, Audi AG, TAS

0   3000 km

A VW – a global company

8 Local actions, global effects

Learn about

In this unit about environmental geography you will learn:

- how to carry out a fieldwork enquiry into the environment
- how to recognise different leisure uses and the possible conflicts of interest between them
- the causes and consequences of the use and misuse of rivers
- how local actions which produce pollution can have global effects.

A Aviemore, Scotland

Fieldwork enquiry

A class of students were doing some geographical fieldwork in Aviemore. Each student was expected to focus their investigation on one of these questions, although they were encouraged to develop further questions as their fieldwork progressed.

- How has the settlement changed over the years?
- What land use is found in the settlement?
- How could the tourist industry in the area be expanded?
- What visitor pressures are there on the settlement?
- What conflicts occur as a result of the land use in this area?

The next four pages show how one student went about his enquiry. You will be asked to decide which enquiry question he chose. First of all, Edward got the most detailed map that he could find. He tried the Internet (use the links at www.heinemann.co.uk/hotlinks).

B Location of Aviemore, Scotland

C Introducing Edward

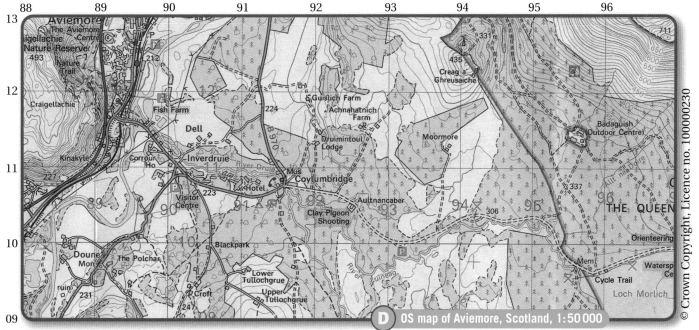

D OS map of Aviemore, Scotland, 1:50 000

© Crown Copyright, Licence no. 100000230

Geography Matters

Case Study

Local actions: Cairngorm funicular railway – debate

The case FOR

The Cairngorm 'funicular railway' opened in December 2001 after years of debate about its effect on the delicate environment of the area.

As well as checking the Internet for information (www.heinemann.co.uk/hotlinks) Edward decided to talk to a representative from the Cairngorm Chairlift Company, to find out the case 'for' the railway; you can see what he found out on this page.

The development was needed to:

- offer a modern, comfortable and reliable method of transport
- run in high winds that stopped the chairlift
- offer better protection to the environment
- promote understanding of the importance of managing access to the area through an exhibition
- allow more visitors to access the area
- create more jobs in the whole area
- give a sustained boost to the local tourist economy.

A Tony, representative of the Cairngorm Chairlift Company

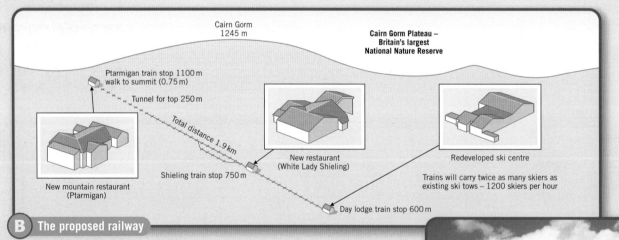

Cairn Gorm
1245 m

Cairn Gorm Plateau –
Britain's largest
National Nature Reserve

Ptarmigan train stop 1100 m
walk to summit (0.75 m)

Tunnel for top 250 m

Total distance 1.9 km

Shieling train stop 750 m

New mountain restaurant
(Ptarmigan)

New restaurant
(White Lady Shieling)

Redeveloped ski centre

Trains will carry twice as many skiers as
existing ski tows – 1200 skiers per hour

Day lodge train stop 600 m

B The proposed railway

	Before development	After opening of railway (estimated)
Cairngorm ski centre income	£3 million	£5 million
Percentage of total income earned in winter months	90%	50%
People travelling up to Ptarmigan Restaurant in summer	50 000	125 000
People walking from Ptarmigan to Cairn Gorm summit in summer	4 000	12 500
Tourist-related jobs in Aviemore area	600	960

D Funicular railway

C Statistics showing impact of proposed development

The case AGAINST

To get a balanced view on the issue Edward decided to check the Internet (www.heinemann.co.uk/hotlinks) and to speak to a number of other users of the mountains to get their views. You can see what he found out on this page.

E Conservationist

> The arctic/alpine environment here is very vulnerable. Crowds of visitors will certainly damage it.

F Hill walker

> I don't think the scheme will make money. It will destroy the environment, and in the end that's what tourists come for.

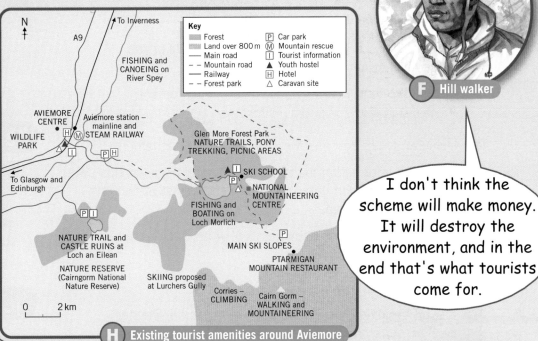

Key

Forest	P Car park
Land over 800 m	M Mountain rescue
Main road	I Tourist information
Mountain road	▲ Youth hostel
Railway	H Hotel
Forest park	△ Caravan site

To Inverness

A9

N

FISHING and CANOEING on River Spey

AVIEMORE CENTRE

Aviemore station – mainline and STEAM RAILWAY

WILDLIFE PARK

To Glasgow and Edinburgh

Glen More Forest Park – NATURE TRAILS, PONY TREKKING, PICNIC AREAS

SKI SCHOOL

NATIONAL MOUNTAINEERING CENTRE

FISHING and BOATING on Loch Morlich

NATURE TRAIL and CASTLE RUINS at Loch an Eilean

NATURE RESERVE (Cairngorm National Nature Reserve)

SKIING proposed at Lurchers Gully

Corries – CLIMBING

MAIN SKI SLOPES

PTARMIGAN MOUNTAIN RESTAURANT

Cairn Gorm – WALKING and MOUNTAINEERING

0   2 km

H Existing tourist amenities around Aviemore

G National Trust Spokesperson

> The scheme is an eyesore and a threat to an important ecosystem.

> Walks and pathways won't cope with thousands of extra feet.

I Bird watcher

> The rare birds in the area – golden eagles, ospreys, ptarmigan – need peace and quiet. They will leave if they are disturbed too often.

J Rambler

Writing up the fieldwork enquiry

Edward was told to write up his field enquiry in four parts:

- Step 1: asking questions – the introduction
- Step 2: gathering information – this section would include primary and secondary data
- Step 3: showing the results – the data is analysed in this section
- Step 4: drawing conclusions – the analysis is used to answer the opening question.

Activities

Step 1 – Writing the introduction

1. Looking at the information that Edward gathered, suggest which enquiry question he chose (see page 133).
   Give reasons for your answer.

2. Using OS map **D** (page 133), describe the *site* of the settlement Aviemore.

3. Choose the term that best describes the settlement:

   single building   village   sub-town   market town.

4. Using an atlas, describe the *situation* of the settlement.

5. Using the information found on the opening pages of this unit, prepare a list which describes briefly the tourist attractions available in Aviemore.

6. Using your answers to activities **1–5**, write the introduction to the fieldwork enquiry.

Step 2 – Gathering the information

7. List all the data that Edward gathered. Decide whether each piece is *primary* or *secondary* data.

8. What other data would he have to collect to complete his enquiry?

Step 3 – Showing the results (data analysis)

9. Choose and illustrate the data gathered by Edward in sketch map **H** (page 135).

Step 4 – Drawing conclusions

10. Using your answer to **9**, write some conclusions that you can make as a result of Edward's fieldwork.

help!

An introduction should be more than just the enquiry question. Successful introductions contain some background information to 'set the scene' in a geographical way.

help!

- Use aerial photograph **A** (page 132) and OS map **D** (page 133) to improve the accuracy of the sketch map, which should appear in the middle of your display.

- Try to use a variety of graphs and diagrams to display the data as well as detailed labels (annotations) and sketches.

- When selecting the data make sure that you link it back to the enquiry question chosen in **1**.

- Try to use the most up-to-date data. Check for any changes made to the proposal before final completion.

What conflicts occur between recreational activities?

Geographers sometimes call places like Aviemore **honeypot** sites.
Such sites attract great numbers of visitors, especially at weekends and in fine
weather. Aviemore attracts most visitors in winter, especially when it snows.

A The competing demands of recreation in Aviemore

B Tourism – for and against

The good points

- Tourism brings money and jobs to areas which otherwise would have little local employment.

- Money from tourism can be used to improve local infrastructure, such as utilities (gas, electricity supply, mains drainage), television reception and mobile phone coverage. Better roads and facilities like shops, public transport and street lighting benefit local people.

The not-so-good points

- Honeypot sites can get so busy that some regulation is needed. If these areas are not carefully controlled, the things that people come to visit may become spoilt and the area will not be visited anymore.

- The tourist season is very short, especially in Britain where the weather is unreliable, so that many of the jobs only last for part of the year.

- Many of the jobs created by the tourist industry are neither highly skilled nor well paid.

The conflict

When people visit an area, they usually need a focus for their recreation. For example, the variety of recreational activities on offer at Aviemore is excellent for attracting visitors. Unfortunately, there can be some conflict between the activities that visitors choose to do.

Activities

1 a Use the speech bubbles on **A** to make a list of some leisure activities in Aviemore.

b Add any other leisure uses that you can think of to your list. You may find OS map **D** on page 133, sketch map **I** on page 135 and other information in this unit useful.

2 Write a short description of the ideal conditions for each of the leisure uses you have listed.

3 Use your answer to question **2** to help you complete a conflict matrix to show how each leisure activity might conflict with other recreational activities. The matrix has been started for you.

4 Taking each recreational activity in turn, give reasons for the pattern of conflicts in your matrix.

5 Because conflict matrices are good at showing which activities cause the most conflicts, planners use them to decide which activities should be most controlled. Based upon your answers to questions **3** and **4**, suggest which recreational activity should be the most controlled in this area.

	Fishing	Walking	Canoeing
Fishing		X	
Walking	X		
Canoeing			

Key: X = some conflict
XX = great conflict
0 = no conflict
? = difficult to decide

Managing leisure activities to reduce conflict

Conflicts may be resolved in a number of ways.

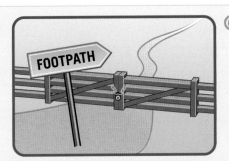

⑤ **Power:** Those activities which are more powerful may 'win the day' because they are either not regulated or earn more money. Recreational activity has to put up with it or disappear.

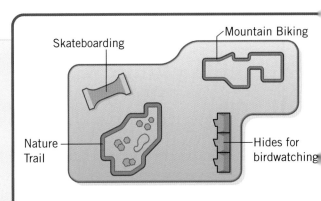

Skateboarding

Mountain Biking

Nature Trail

Hides for birdwatching

⑤ **Time solutions:** Conflicts can be reduced by allowing recreational users to operate at different times of the day or year.

Skateboarders banned from park – council plan purpose-built ramps

⑤ **Buying off:** The losers in a conflict may be given some form of compensation to make up for their loss. For example, they may be given somewhere else to use.

⑤ **Zoning:** Different activities can be given different areas in which to operate, so that conflicts are kept to a minimum.

⑤ **Amelioration** (lessening the bad effects): The activities of the 'winners' in a conflict are controlled so as to minimise their bad effects.

Activities

⑥ Suggest how each of the following decisions might affect the lives of the residents and other leisure users in the Aviemore area.

  a Allowing loud music to be broadcast from one of the pubs.

  b Allowing small power boats on the loch.

  c Closing down the public car park.

  d Stopping people using the footpaths in the area.

⑦ On the basis of your answers to **6**, put the four decisions in order of the environmental effect they might have. Write brief reasons for your answer.

⑧ Choose one of the decisions in **6** and suggest five ways in which the conflict could be resolved.

⑨ Produce a labelled sketch map of the area in which you suggest a full management plan to minimise all the potential conflicts.

help!

Try to think of the effects that might result from these decisions and how they might affect the activities of other people.

help!

Think about how activities could be zoned:

✪ to minimise disruption of the lives of residents

✪ to reduce conflicts with other recreational activities.

How do people use and misuse rivers?

Case Study

Rhine River Basin and fresh water pollution

The River Rhine is one of the world's greatest commercial rivers. It flows through many important countries in the industrial heartland of Europe: from the Swiss mountains the Rhine's course goes past and into the Bodensee. From there its course marks first the Swiss–German border and then the French–German border. It finally flows through Germany and into the Netherlands. The Rhine basin is very densely populated as a result of highly developed industry, trade and agriculture, as well as a dense network of motorways and railways. Demands on the river have therefore been very heavy. Although the Rhine is much cleaner than it used to be, pollution from manufacturing industry, from farming and from sewage remains a major international problem.

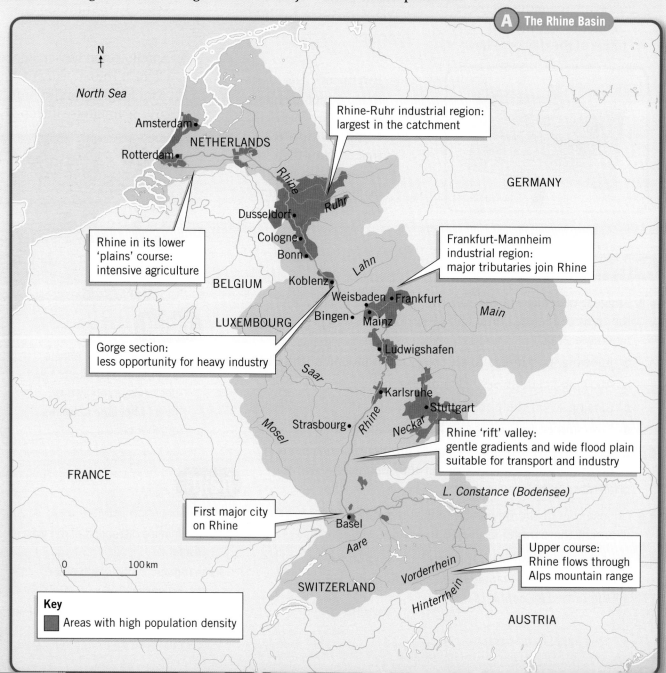

A The Rhine Basin

Rhine-Ruhr industrial region: largest in the catchment

Rhine in its lower 'plains' course: intensive agriculture

Frankfurt-Mannheim industrial region: major tributaries join Rhine

Gorge section: less opportunity for heavy industry

Rhine 'rift' valley: gentle gradients and wide flood plain suitable for transport and industry

First major city on Rhine

Upper course: Rhine flows through Alps mountain range

North Sea
Amsterdam
NETHERLANDS
Rotterdam
Rhine
Ruhr
GERMANY
Dusseldorf
Cologne
Bonn
Lahn
BELGIUM
Koblenz
Weisbaden • Frankfurt
Main
Bingen • Mainz
LUXEMBOURG
Ludwigshafen
Saar
Karlsruhe
Stuttgart
Mosel
Strasbourg • Rhine
Neckar
L. Constance (Bodensee)
FRANCE
Basel
Aare
Vorderrhein
SWITZERLAND
Hinterrhein
AUSTRIA

0   100 km

Key
Areas with high population density

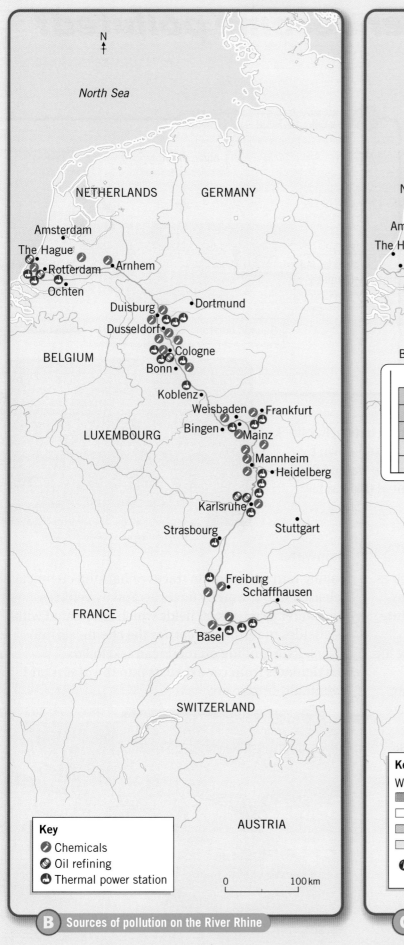

B Sources of pollution on the River Rhine

Key
- 🖋 Chemicals
- ◎ Oil refining
- ⛽ Thermal power station

0   100 km

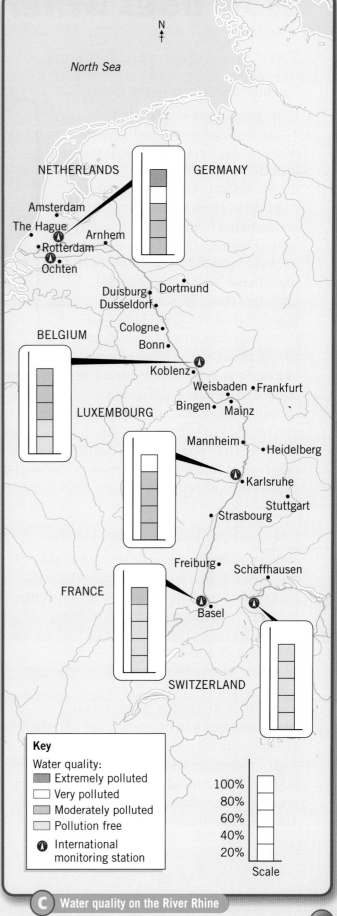

C Water quality on the River Rhine

Key
Water quality:
- ▨ Extremely polluted
- ☐ Very polluted
- ▨ Moderately polluted
- ☐ Pollution free
- ⊙ International monitoring station

100%
80%
60%
40%
20%

Scale

How does water become polluted?

Fresh water pollution

Too many nutrients in the water

Blue-green algae are naturally occurring organisms which feed off nutrients in rivers and lakes. Algae are broken down by organisms further up the food chain and so, under natural conditions, there is a balance. When waste matter from farming, industry or sewage enters a river it causes a big increase in **nutrients** like nitrates and phosphates, which stimulate the growth of algae. These nutrients, together with strong sunlight, give favourable conditions for an **algal bloom** to occur. The algae multiply so fast that a green scum appears on the surface of the water and toxins (poisons) are produced. Toxins are dangerous to fish, livestock and humans. When the algae die they are broken down by bacteria. The bacteria use up the oxygen in the water, killing other water creatures. Nutrient enrichment of this kind is called **eutrophication**.

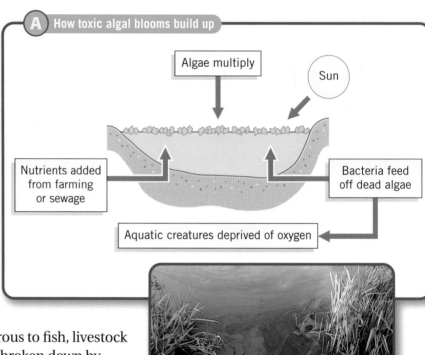

A How toxic algal blooms build up

Algae multiply

Sun

Nutrients added from farming or sewage

Bacteria feed off dead algae

Aquatic creatures deprived of oxygen

B Green scum appears on the surface of a lake

The consequences of industrial waste

Factories can discharge heavy metals such as magnesium, zinc and copper into rivers as part of the waste they produce. Rivers **dilute** this waste, but large quantities of heavy metals are toxic. They poison much of the life in both fresh and salt water.

Some chemicals dumped into rivers are not broken down naturally because they are man-made. Many detergents are not **biodegradable** and tiny quantities of these chemicals build up in animals over time. In high concentrations they can kill. This process is called **bioaccumulation**. The situation gets worse when predators at the top of the food chain eat affected animals.

Rainwater

Falling rain may contain traces of harmful chemicals released into the air by factories and by vehicles. Rainwater that runs off fields which are treated with pesticides or fertilisers, carries the chemicals into rivers. Rain landing on roads can take oil or **particulates** from car exhausts into the drains and eventually into rivers.

C Oil and particulates from vehicles drain eventually into rivers

Birds suffer from oil pollution in three ways. It kills their food, and also clogs their feathers so they are no longer waterproof and the birds get cold. When the birds try to clean themselves, they are poisoned by the oil.

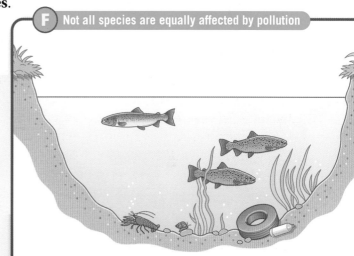
D An oiled sea-bird

Thermal pollution

Factories often use water from rivers for cooling. When the water is returned to the river it is warmer, and this can have environmental impacts. Some bacteria may be killed by just slight increases in temperature. This is called **thermal pollution**.

E A coal-fired power station

Indicators of pollution

Fish swimming through a river may not be much affected by pollution. But creatures that live on the bed of a river can show pollution levels very well. If conditions are wrong they cannot simply swim away. So these are sometimes called **indicator species**.

F Not all species are equally affected by pollution

Activities

1. Make a word bank of key words for this unit. Start with the words in bold on this page. Add any key words you have learned from pages 132–142.

2. Salmon need to travel up river to spawn (lay eggs). They must find a place with good quality, shallow water and a river bed made up of *gravel*, not *silt*. Imagine that you are a salmon making your way up the River Rhine from the sea. Describe your journey, noting any changes in water quality that you come across – try to explain these pollution events. Looking up the international IKSR website through www.heinemann.co.uk/hotlinks might help you. (ICT)

3. a Take each of the sources of pollution on the River Rhine and explain how they affect the river.

   b Draw a scale of pollution on the River Rhine like the one below. Label the uses of the river onto the scale according to the pollution they cause.

help!

Choose from: power station, sewage works downstream of major settlement, intensive agriculture, industry from the Ruhr valley. Your atlas may help you with more.

```
    0    1    2    3    4    5    6    7    8    9    10
    |----|----|----|----|----|----|----|----|----|----|
  Least pollution                            Most pollution
```

   c Explain your answer to **3b**.

4. Using the evidence of changes in water quality from map **C** on page 141, explain how rivers clean themselves as they flow towards the sea.

'Behold the sea, the teeming sea ...'

Most river water, and any pollution that it carries, ends up in the sea. The sea has always been used as a dumping ground. In the past people thought the world's oceans were so vast they could absorb any pollution they received. Today some seas are at serious risk from pollution; one example is the North Sea.

Seawater food chains

A Plankton are tiny, single-celled plants which float around in the top layer of the sea — they form the heart of the food web

B There may be many millions of copepods in each cubic metre of water — these graze off the phytoplankton

C Floating in the sea's currents, jellyfish trap copepods and anything else that swims against their long trailing tentacles

D Starfish and sea-urchins feed on a wide variety of shellfish — they are 'keystone' species that control the populations of some other species

E Herring and mackerel are surface fish which form shoals for safety from predators

F Great grey seals eat a wide variety of fish, crustaceans and sea-urchins

G Killer whales feed on large fish, dolphins, seals and even other whales, but they are not known to attack humans

H About 90 000 gannets come to the North Sea to breed. They enjoy a diet of larger fish

I The wolf fish crushes whelks, scallops, sea-urchins and crabs with its powerful jaws

While the North Sea is one of the world's largest coastal seas, it only contains 1 per cent of the Earth's sea water. It is almost entirely surrounded by land, with the southern part narrowing to a **strait** of water 35 kilometres wide between Dover and Calais. As it is on the **continental shelf**, it is a mainly shallow sea between 25 and 55 metres deep. In the north, the Norwegian Trench is over 200 metres deep.

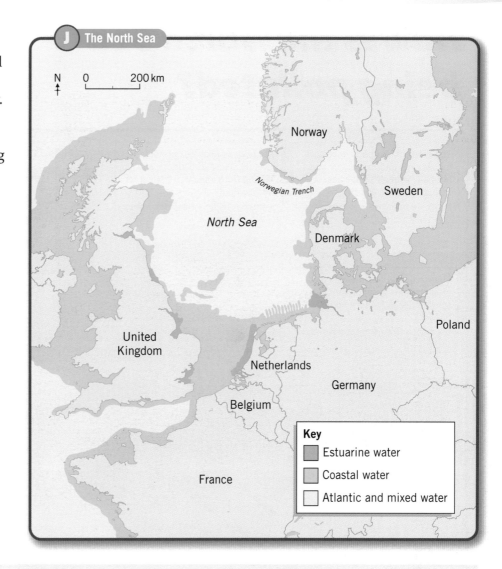

J The North Sea

N

0   200 km

Norway

Norwegian Trench

Sweden

North Sea

Denmark

Poland

United Kingdom

Netherlands

Germany

Belgium

France

Key
Estuarine water
Coastal water
Atlantic and mixed water

Activities

1 Write a short paragraph to introduce the North Sea. Include information on its location and the scale of the area, as well as an outline of the Sea's physical and human geography.

2 Use the location map and an atlas to list all the distinct environments that exist for wildlife within the North Sea.

3 Using the photographs on the opposite page, construct a food web diagram to show the feeding levels in the North Sea. Start by copying the diagram on the right.

4 **Extension**

Navigate the website for Ball State University's Exploring Ecosystems at www.heinemann.co.uk/hotlinks to extend your web diagram. ICT

5 What factors make the North Sea so at risk from pollution? Extend your writing to compare the pollution potential of the North Sea with that of the Bristol Channel.

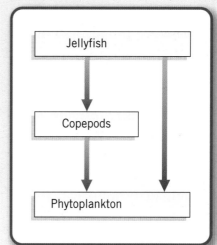

Jellyfish

Copepods

Phytoplankton

How is the North Sea being polluted?

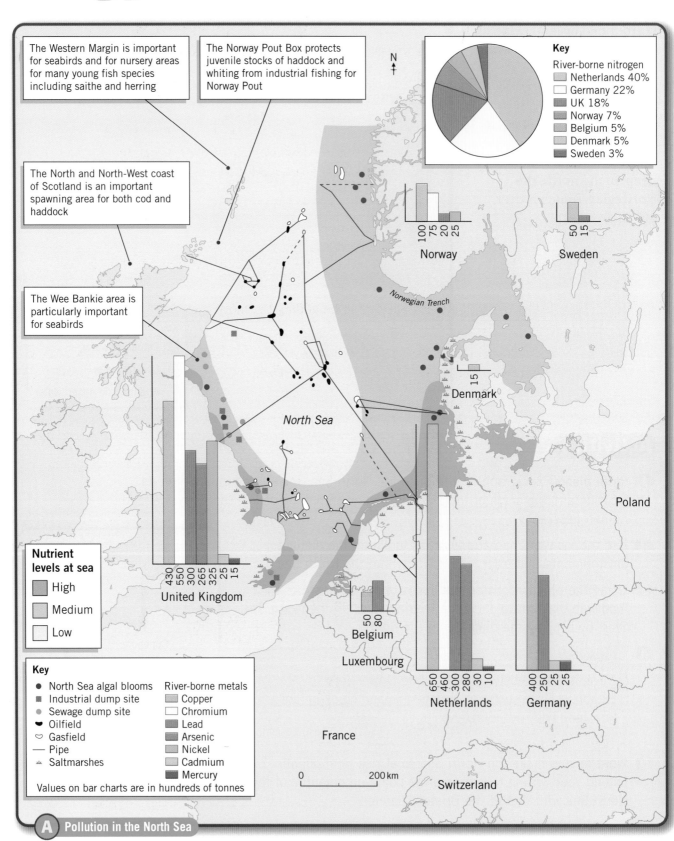

The Western Margin is important for seabirds and for nursery areas for many young fish species including saithe and herring

The Norway Pout Box protects juvenile stocks of haddock and whiting from industrial fishing for Norway Pout

The North and North-West coast of Scotland is an important spawning area for both cod and haddock

The Wee Bankie area is particularly important for seabirds

Key
River-borne nitrogen
- Netherlands 40%
- Germany 22%
- UK 18%
- Norway 7%
- Belgium 5%
- Denmark 5%
- Sweden 3%

N

Norway
100 75 20 25

Sweden
50 15

Norwegian Trench

Denmark
15

North Sea

Poland

United Kingdom
430 550 300 265 325 25 15

Nutrient levels at sea
- High
- Medium
- Low

Belgium
50 80

Luxembourg

Netherlands
650 460 300 280 30 10

Germany
400 250 25 25

France

0   200 km

Switzerland

Key
- ● North Sea algal blooms
- ■ Industrial dump site
- ● Sewage dump site
- ❤ Oilfield
- ♡ Gasfield
- — Pipe
- ⚓ Saltmarshes

River-borne metals
- Copper
- Chromium
- Lead
- Arsenic
- Nickel
- Cadmium
- Mercury

Values on bar charts are in hundreds of tonnes

A Pollution in the North Sea

Europe's dustbin!

Over 50 million people live close to the shores of the North Sea. It is surrounded by some of the world's most industrialised nations. There is very great stress on the North Sea as it is **exploited** for a number of conflicting uses including:

- intensive use of fish stocks for food
- extraction of water to cool power stations
- extraction of sand and gravel for the building industry
- extraction of natural gas and oil

- as an important shipping route
- as an area for relaxation
- as a huge dump for the unwanted rubbish produced by advanced industrial nations.

The pattern of currents means that it often takes three years for any waste to circulate back into the Atlantic Ocean. The North Sea has become one of the dirtiest and most polluted seas in the world.

Activities

1. Using map **A**, list all the causes of North Sea pollution. Try to name the country that is the chief polluter for each cause that you list.

2. Try to explain why the Netherlands appears to be adding the most river-borne heavy metals into the North Sea.

3. Explain how the sources of pollution that you have listed could affect each of the creatures mentioned on page 144. Put the creatures in order of danger and explain your decisions.

4. Use map **A** to identify the main areas within the North Sea region which have the most stress from water pollution. You might want to draw a sketch map.

5. Explain at least two effects on the North Sea environment that would result from each of these measures.

   a An international ban on dumping rubbish at sea.

   b Using larger tankers to transport oil in the North Sea.

   c Making companies clean their waste products before they are put into rivers.

   d Heavy taxes on oil companies who pollute the sea.

   e Giving each country a strict quota on the amount of fish that can be caught.

   f Giving extra money to farmers to produce organic food.

6. Suggest any further measures that you think should be introduced to bring pollution in the North Sea under control.

7. Suggest why all progress to clean up the North Sea must be through international agreement. Which nations, in your view, should be involved in making these decisions?

help!

Ideas could include;
- using satellite imagery
- changing techniques in the fishing industry
- encouraging renewable sources of electricity production
- international co-operation
- controlling air pollution
- building cleaner vehicles.

Global effects

Case Study

What is the future of Antarctica?

Activities

You are going to use the information on pages 148–153 to conduct a full enquiry using secondary sources. Your enquiry will be divided into the familiar sections:

🌀 **Step 1: asking questions**
– some questions have been suggested on this page. Try to break down your main question into smaller questions to help you plan out your work. The introduction should include background information, including the location of the area; you will find suitable material on page 149.

🌀 **Step 2: collecting information**
– this section will include secondary data, which you can find on pages 150–153. You can find more secondary information by conducting a web enquiry using a search engine.

🌀 **Step 3: showing the results**
– the data is analysed in this section. You will have a great deal of information on Antarctica – pick out only the relevant parts.

🌀 **Step 4: drawing conclusions**
– at this point you draw the enquiry to a close by answering the opening enquiry question based upon your analysis.

How can Antarctica be conserved and managed to sustain its environment?

Why is Antarctica a fragile environment?

Why is Antarctica under threat?

How have the activities of the industrialised nations affected Antarctica?

Which parts of Antarctica are threatened with most damage?

A

Antarctica: the last wilderness

The very harsh and difficult environment of Antarctica means that the continent is not threatened by development to the same degree as other places in the world. It is, however, a very fragile environment for a number of reasons.

- Because of the intense cold, the usual processes which cause matter to decay and break down naturally only occur very slowly (see **C**).

- Food webs in this area depend upon one or two key species (see **D**).

- Conditions are so harsh that animals can breed successfully only in one or two areas; these areas are densely populated with animals, which have unique ecosystems.

ICT idea More information can be found on websites for Environmental Action and Antarctica at www.heinemann.co.uk/hotlinks

C Although this husky has been dead for 85 years, its carcass is preserved by the cold, dry conditions

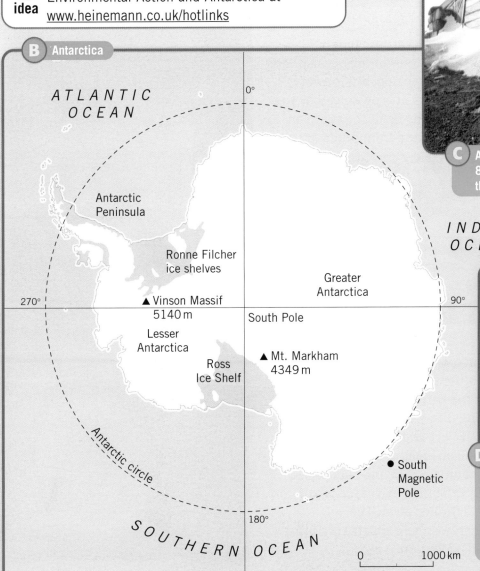

B Antarctica

ATLANTIC OCEAN

0°

Antarctic Peninsula

INDIAN OCEAN

Ronne Filcher ice shelves

Greater Antarctica

270°

▲ Vinson Massif 5140 m

90°

South Pole

Lesser Antarctica

Ross Ice Shelf

▲ Mt. Markham 4349 m

Antarctic circle

● South Magnetic Pole

180°

SOUTHERN OCEAN

0   1000 km

D Krill form the food for five species of whale, three species of seal, twenty species of fish, three species of squid and numerous birds, including penguins. Krill are fished by mankind and although they are sustainable at present, there are local shortages

How does global air pollution affect Antarctica?

The carbon dioxide issue

Greenhouse gases (GHGs) in the atmosphere allow the Sun's rays in but trap radiated heat from the Earth. Carbon dioxide is a gas that occurs naturally and helps to control the Earth's temperature. However, over the past 200 years the burning of fossil fuels has increased the amount of carbon dioxide in the atmosphere. This has led to global warming by the **accelerated greenhouse effect**. A warmer atmosphere is likely to melt parts of the Antarctic ice cap. This could have global effects on sea levels and on ocean currents.

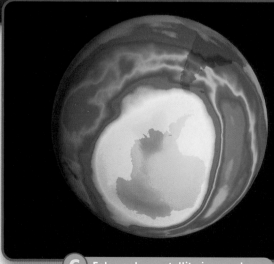

E Burning fossil fuels releases CO_2 into the atmosphere

F Herds of cattle release CH_4 into the atmosphere

All about methane

Methane (CH_4) occurs in much smaller quantities in the atmosphere than carbon dioxide, but is a very powerful GHG. It is produced by rice grown in paddy fields, by cattle, in rubbish tips, and from other sources.

CFCs and the ozone problem

Ozone (O_3) is a poisonous substance which causes harmful pollution at ground level. On the other hand, ozone in the stratosphere, 25 kilometres above the Earth's surface, is vital for controlling the amount of incoming ultra-violet radiation. Gases like **chlorofluorocarbons (CFCs)** break down this protective shield. This effect is worse in areas of intense cold, especially in springtime. In most countries CFC production is strictly controlled, but many CFCs will only be released when appliances like old refrigerators are thrown away. The destruction of ozone in the upper atmosphere above Antarctica is one indicator of the effects of this pollution.

G False colour satellite image shows ozone 'hole' over the Antarctic

NO$_x$ and SO$_2$

Sulphur dioxide (SO$_2$) and nitrogen oxides (NO$_x$) are given off by coal-fired power stations and car exhausts. They reach the ground via rainfall or by dry deposition. Their effect is often felt further away as chimney stacks are now built increasingly high. They cause **acid rain**, which not only kills trees but causes streams and lakes to become 'dead' and lifeless.

H Pollution from vehicle exhausts can become locked into ice sheets

Lead and other heavy metals

Lead and other heavy metals are often found in vehicle exhausts and in the smoke released by factories. They can become trapped in the polar ice sheets. In Antarctica there are traces of heavy metals and organic toxins, which have been carried from the inhabited parts of the world. These will be returned to the environment if the ice melts.

I Acid rain can kill trees

J Dead lakes can look very beautiful but their clear water often means a lack of biological activity

Is the Antarctic ice sheet getting thinner?

Massive iceberg peels away from Antarctic ice shelf

A monster iceberg called B-15, 290 km long by 30 km wide, has broken away from Antarctica's Ross Ice Shelf. At 11 000 square kilometres in area, it is about half the size of Wales and looms 50 metres (fifteen storeys) above the water. Although very large icebergs occasionally calve from ice sheets, this one is thought to be the largest one ever.

K News report, March 2000

L Ice breaking off ice shelf

Cracks in the Antarctic ice shelf have been closely observed since the coming of remote sensing by satellites. The break off of this iceberg is believed to be part of a normal process. Over time, the ice sheet maintains a balance between growth and losses like this.

The recent calving of massive icebergs is a clear sign that global warming is destroying the ice sheets of the western Antarctic. Devastating sea level rises as well as complex changes to the world's climate are now inevitable. Drastic reductions to GHGs are needed now.

M Two conflicting views on the Antarctic ice sheet

The loss of ice shelves from Antarctica

Are the large cracks which have appeared in the ice sheets around Antarctica part of a natural process or an effect of global warming? The *causes* are not certain. Some scientists believe that the *effects* of enormous quantities of ice melting in the Southern Ocean will change our climate. No one today can predict what will happen exactly, but these suggestions have been made:

- The Ross and Ronne ice shelves are like two big plugs which support the ice on the main part of Antarctica. If they melt the whole of the sheet will become unstable.

- The melting of ice shelves, made up of floating ice, will have no effect on world sea levels. However, if lots of cold water is suddenly released into the oceans, this may affect the pattern of ocean currents.

- Ocean currents are important in transferring heat from the Equator to the Poles. They stop the world overheating.

Larsen ice shelf — Massive loss of ice

Ronne ice shelf

Ross ice shelf — together with the Ronne ice shelf act as two giant 'plugs' supporting ice on the Antarctic landmass

If the Ronne and Ross ice shelves both melt (1), it will be as if two plugs are pulled on the massive layer of ice sitting on top of the land, allowing some of it to slip off (2). Once in the relatively warmer water, melting will be speeded up.

N Antarctic meltdown

- Most of Antarctica has had a stable climate for the past 40 years. It is only the Antarctic peninsula that is warming at a rate of two to three times the global average.

- If there is less ice on the Poles, then fewer of the Sun's rays will be reflected back into space.

Other stresses on the environment

Mining

Mining in Antarctica has been banned for at least the next 50 years through an international agreement called the Protocol on Environmental Protection to the Antarctic Treaty. There are, however, many valuable deposits of iron, oil and gas. In the future, when these minerals run out in other parts of the world, the pressure for mining here will become very strong.

Impact of scientists

There are only ever about 10 000 scientists on an area 58 times the size of Britain. All rubbish and waste must be removed from the continent, and it is very expensive to dispose of. In such cold temperatures, the normal natural processes of decomposition are very slow.

Tourism

Increasingly Antarctic cruises are being offered to tourists who are keen to enjoy the wonders of the continent. There are fears that tourists will cause pressure on the fragile vegetation and disturb the breeding grounds of animals.

Review and reflect

What future is there for the Aviemore environment?

Scenario 1: Sustainable development

Agreement on stopping global warming might mean unpopular controls, including some on leisure activities. This course of action could provide a better long-term future for all developments.

Scenario 2: Uncontrolled development

Without agreements between land users, uncontrolled economic development could produce great advantages for a few in the short term. In the long term, it could bring disaster.

Activities

1 Update your word bank so that it covers the whole unit. This will help you with the final activities.

2 Read the headlines below. For each headline:

a Suggest whether the change is local, regional or global in scale.

b Explain what might have caused the change to happen and suggest what effects it might produce.

c Suggest how each change would affect you. Give your reasons.

> **help!**
>
> Think of all the possibilities – some might be good but some might be bad.

Ozone hole over the Arctic bigger than ever

North Sea fishermen forced to catch smaller fish

Global temperatures rise and rise!

Global warming brings more storms to Britain

Cheap fuel for the British motorist: fuel protestors triumphant!

The Arctic Ocean becomes a major shipping route

Maldive Islands finally disappear under the Indian Ocean

Overharvesting endangers krill supplies

European governments agree to control factory emissions

Breakthrough! Cheap and practical electric car available soon

---

3 Look carefully at cartoons **A** and **B**. They show two very different predictions of what might happen in the future.

a Describe each cartoon and contrast the two predictions.

b Try to explain why the two cartoonists have different views of the future.

c In your own view, which is the more likely prediction? Give reasons for your viewpoint.

Glossary

Accelerated greenhouse effect   The increased warming of the Earth caused by humans burning fossil fuels. This leads to a build-up of carbon dioxide in the atmosphere, so less heat escapes into space.

Acid rain   Rain that contains dilute sulphuric or nitric acid. The acids come from air pollution and are dissolved by the rain as it falls to earth.

Arterial roads   Main roads which link important towns.

Atmosphere   The layer of gases surrounding the Earth.

Automated   When machines are used instead of people to make things.

Bioaccumulation   The process where chemicals build up in the bodies of animals over time.

Biodegradable   Able to be broken down naturally and harmlessly, for example by bacteria.

Blue-green algae   Algae are small, simple plants that live in water. Blue–green algae increase rapidly in water which is rich in nutrients, especially in strong sunlight.

Centralised   Where power is held by a few people in the capital city.

Chlorofluorocarbon (CFC)   A chemical used in some aerosols and fridges which damages the Earth's ozone layer.

Choropleth map   A map using density shading for particular groups. It is also known as a **density map**.

Commodities   Useful things such as cotton, often used for trade.

Communications   Roads, railways and other ways of linking people and places, including telephones and computers.

Communist government   A government which believes in everyone sharing the country's work and property.

Components   The parts that make up something; for example, a car is made up of thousands of different components.

Conflict   Where groups of people have different ideas about how an area should be used. These conflicts can be shown on a conflict matrix.

Consumers   People who buy goods or services.

Continental shelf   The shallow part of the sea around a continent.

Crude oil   Petroleum in its natural liquid state as it emerges from the ground, before refining.

Deep sea trench   A deep trench or underwater valley formed where continental crust meets oceanic crust.

Democratic government   A government which is voted into office by the people.

Density map   see **choropleth map**.

Development indicators   Ways in which development is measured.

Dispersed   Scattered.

Drought   A period of low rainfall, often over many years.

Economic development   The success of an area or country at producing useful goods.

Ecotourism   Tourism which is in the environment but doesn't damage it.

Equatorial   A type of climate found near the Equator.

Eutrophication   This process can happen in water rich in nutrients. Algae and bacteria grow rapidly and use up all the oxygen, killing other water creatures.

Evapotranspiration   The total loss of water by evaporation from the soil and other surfaces plus water released from plants.

Exploited   When a natural resource is used by people.

Exports   Goods and services sold by one country to another.

Extensive ranching   Cattle farming in which there are only a few cattle per hectare.

Factor   The reason for something, or something which brings about a result.

Fault   A break in the rocks caused by movements in the Earth's crust.

Feeder roads   Small roads which link into main roads.

Focus   The point beneath the Earth's crust where an earthquake starts.

Food chain   A cycle that begins with green plants that take their energy from sunlight, continuing with organisms that eat these plants, to other organisms that consume the plant-eating organisms, then to decomposers that break down the dead bodies of those organisms so that they can be used as soil nutrients by plants, starting the cycle again.

Frequently asked questions (FAQs)   The part of a website that provides answers to the questions that people ask most often.

Greenhouse effect   A natural process where carbon dioxide in the atmosphere prevents some of the Earth's heat from escaping back into space. It keeps the Earth warm enough to live on.

Head office   The headquarters of a company, where the company's top bosses work.

Hierarchy   A series of geographical features that build up: for example, a small village, a market town, a large town, a city.

Honeypot site   Tourist attraction which attracts many visitors, especially during public holidays and the summer months.

Hydro-electric power   A way of generating electricity by using the force of water to turn a turbine.

Indicator species   Creatures which are very sensitive to pollution. If these creatures are found in water they can show the level of pollution there.

Interdependent   People or countries who depend on each other.

Invest   To put money into a business.

Kanji   A type of Japanese writing.

Latitude   Distance north or south of the Equator measured in degrees.

Layer shading   A method of showing the height of land using a series of colours.

Lowland   Land between 0 and 100 metres above sea level, usually fairly flat.

Manufacturers   Companies or people who make goods.

Market   The place where goods are sold; for example, the main market for Rover cars is in Britain and the rest of Europe.

Media   Newspapers, TV and radio all together.

Meteorologist   A scientist who studies the weather.

Methane (CH_4)   A gas produced by industry, car exhausts and cattle. It is a more powerful greenhouse gas than carbon dioxide.

Monitor   To check or observe something at regular intervals to see if there are any changes. In earthquake areas, for example, scientists use seismographs to detect the first signs of ground movement.

Multinational companies   Large companies which operate in many countries around the world.

Natural fibres   Threads or material made from cotton, wool or silk.

Nutrients   Food for plants or animals; nutrients are absorbed to help plants and animals survive and grow.

Ocean current   A flow of warm or cold water.

Open policy   The Chinese government's decision to open up China to foreign trade and investment.

Ozone (O_3)   A gas found in the upper layers of the Earth's atmosphere.

Ozone layer   The layer of the upper atmosphere, from about 12 to 50 kilometres above the Earth's surface, that protects the Earth from harmful radiation from the Sun.

Particulates   Tiny specks of dust that can form the centre around which raindrops form.

Perceptions   How we see or think about something or somebody.

Photosynthesis   Green plants use the energy of sunlight to convert carbon dioxide and water into energy which they use for growth. At the same time they release oxygen into the air.

Plateau   A large, fairly flat area of highland.

Prefecture   A local government area in Japan, similar to a county in Britain

Primary productivity   The rate at which green plants store energy as carbohydrates to be consumed by other organisms.

Refined oil   Oil in a form that can be used in, for example, homes and cars. It is made by removing the impurities from crude oil.

Selva   Rainforest.

Site   The place where a factory or town is built.

Stereotyping   Having a fixed idea about what a country or people are like; often a negative idea.

Strait   A narrow strip of water between two pieces of land.

Sustainability   The wise use of resources today, so that people in the future can still use them. Resources used in this way are **sustainable**.

Sustainable tourism   Tourism which doesn't damage the environment or people's lifestyles.

Sweatshop   A factory where people have to work very long hours, often in difficult or dangerous conditions, for low wages.

Technopole   A French centre for science and high-tech industry.

Tectonic plates   The Earth's crust is made up of huge slabs called tectonic plates.

Temperature   How hot or cold a place is.

Thermal pollution   A rise in the temperature of water caused by waste water from factories or power stations.

Trade   Buying, selling or exchanging goods, often between countries.

Trade surplus   When a country exports more goods and services than it imports.

Trading partners   Two or more countries who trade together.

Transnational Corporations (TNCs)   Large companies that operate in many countries around the world.

Transport   Carry; for example, rock fragments that have been eroded are removed or transported by the sea, wind, ice or rivers.

Upland   Land above 100 metres above sea level, usually hills or mountains.

Ward   A small area (political division) in a town or city.

Index

accelerated greenhouse effect 150, 156
acid rain 151, 156
adult literacy rates 37, 59
agriculture 72–3
algal bloom 142
Amazonia 54, 64
Antarctica 148–53
anticyclones 16
area 7
arterial roads 60, 156
atmosphere 156
'Auld Reekie' 12
averages 36
Aviemore 137–8, 154

balance of trade 106
bar charts 123
bioaccumulation 142, 156
Blackpool 116
blue-green algae 142, 156
BMW 128–9
Brazil 44–54
    regions 50–2
British Isles 6

Cairngorm funicular railway 134–6
call centres 19
car industry 122–31
case studies
    Antarctica 148
    Brazil 50
    car industry 126–9
    China 94
    environmental geography 134–6
    Japan 104
    Kenya 35, 38
    manufacturing 74
    rivers 140–1
    tourism 78, 116
cattle ranching 61
CFCs see chlorofluorocarbons
China 89–98, 106–8, 110
chlorofluorocarbons (CFCs) 150, 156
choropleth map 156
clear-cut forestry 40
climate 14

coal 79
Communist government 99, 156
components 156
conflict matrix 67
consumers 85
continental shelf 145, 156
councils 9
Cowley 126–7
crude oil 156
cultural links 109

DCR see development compass rose
deep sea trench 156
democratic government 156
density map 156
depressions 16
developed country 56–7
development 24–7
    Brazil 60–4
    inequalities 34
    mapping 32
    progress 37
    projects 41
    quality of life 28–9
    regional variations 30–1
development compass rose (DCR) 29, 57
development indicators 33
drought 53, 156
Dunoon 13

earthquakes 97, 103
economic activities 69, 70, 113
economic development 58, 156
ecotourism 120, 156
Edinburgh 12
employment 17, 71
energy consumption 59
energy resources 79
environmental geography 132
European Union 86
eutrophication 142, 156
evapotranspiration 156
exports 84, 106, 125, 156

facts 5
FAQs see frequently asked questions
feeder roads 60, 157
fieldwork 133
fire 97
floods 97, 103
food chains 144, 157
food webs 149
Forestry Stewardship Council 40
France 68–87
frequently asked questions (FAQs) 157
fronts 16

gas 80
GHGs see greenhouse gases
Glasgow 12, 19
global warming 152–3
GNP see Gross National Product
government, China 99
Great Britain 6
greenhouse gases (GHGs) 150
Gross National Product (GNP) 31, 59

HDI see Human Development Index
heavy metals 151
HEP see hydroelectric power
herbicides 61
honeypot sites 137, 157
Hong Kong 99, 107
Human Development Index (HDI) 31
hydroelectric power (HEP) 64, 80, 157

images 10, 11, 46
imports 85, 106
IMR see infant mortality rate
indicator species 143, 157
industry 17–18
infant mortality rate (IMR) 59
international trade 84–5
Inverness 13
invisible exports 106
islands 8

Japan 89–91, 100–6, 108–10

Kenya 35, 38

landslides 103
latitude 157
layer shading 157
lead 151
Less Economically Developed
    Countries (LEDCs) 25
life expectancy 37, 59
local government 9

manufacturing industry 74
maps 8
media 94, 104, 157
methane 150, 157
mining 64, 153
More Economically Developed
    Countries (MEDCs) 25
mountains 8

nitrogen oxides 151
North Sea 145–7
nuclear power 81–3
nutrients 157

oil 80
opinions 5
ozone 150, 157

perceptions 5, 25, 89
photosynthesis 157
plateau 52, 96, 157
political map 9
pollution 80, 142–7
population 7
population growth 59
poverty 26
prefectures 100, 157
primary activities 69

quality of life 28

rainforest 55
ratios 34
regions 98
Rhine River 140–1
rivers 8, 140–1
road building 60

safe water 59
St Lucia 118–19
savanna 52
scattergraphs 15
seawater food chains 144
secondary activities 69
selvas 55, 158
settlements 9
standard of living 28
statistics 34
stereotypes 89, 105
Stornoway 13
sulphur dioxide 151
sustainable development
    40–2, 55
sustainable tourism 120, 158

technopoles 74–5
thermal pollution 143, 158
timeline 65
TNCs see transnational
    corporations
tourism 112–21
    Antarctic 153
    France 76–8
    Scotland 20–2
trade 84–5, 106, 158
transnational corporations
    (TNCs) 158
transport 60
typhoons 103

under-five mortality rate
    (U5MR) 37
unemployment 71
United Kingdom 6
United Kingdom car industry
    124
upland areas 8

visible exports 106
volcanoes 103

water features 8
water pollution 142–3
weather 14–17
wind farms 27
World Bank 33
World Trade Organisation
    (WTO) 106
written reports 111, 136

zoning 139